THE PERSONAL JOURNEY
OF A
BLACK COMMON SENSE CONSERVATIVE

By Carl Pittman

Copyright © 2014 by Carl Pittman

The Personal Journey of a Black Common Sense Conservative
by Carl Pittman

Printed in the United States of America

ISBN 9781629525181

All rights reserved solely by the author. The author guarantees all contents are original and do not infringe upon the legal rights of any other person or work. No part of this book may be reproduced in any form without the permission of the author. The views expressed in this book are not necessarily those of the publisher.

Unless otherwise indicated, Bible quotations are taken from the New King James Version (NKJV). Copyright © 1982 by Thomas Nelson, Inc. Used by permission. All rights reserved.

www.xulonpress.com

THANK YOU

When I decided to write this book I thought it would be rather easy; however, this process has taken almost two years and hundreds of hours. I could never have completed this project without a few very important people.

First I would like to thank my wife, Kristi for her ongoing support and encouragement to complete this book. Men, I cannot understate the importance of a caring and supportive wife while trying to accomplish anything be it running for office or writing a book.

To my son, Justin, daughter, Noel and my grandson, Brennan I cannot think of anything in this world more important to me than the three of you. I am endeavoring to make some small difference in the world that I will leave to you. Never forget that you are where you are and who you are because of those who came before you. Thank you for allowing me to love you.

To Richard Dillon and Bill Kneer: These two fine Christian men have over the past few years proven to be not only great friends and supporters, but I have come to think of them as my brothers. Richard with his photography, computer, technical and editing skills made what could have been a nightmare much more bearable. Bill would tell you that he is the best looking guy in the room; I cannot confirm that fact, however, I can confirm that there is no better or more loyal friend. To both of you, Richard and Bill thank you from the bottom of my heart for all of your help and support over the years.

There are so many people that I must thank for their ongoing support during my 2012 race for Harris County Sheriff. Mr. Lee Cook, Chairman and founder of Phonoscope Communications and his absolute demand for constitutional compliance should be followed by every elected official in this country. My good friend, Sam Malone also of Phonoscope Communications and host of the Sam Malone Show on AM 1070 "The Answer" is one of the strongest conservative voices in the region and allows me to frequently contribute to the show.

Mr. Charles T. Fogarty, the owner and operator of Steamboat House Steakhouse in Houston, Texas who continues to serve as my campaign Treasurer. Thank you for your ongoing support and friendship.

Mary Sergesketter, my campaign consultant who has become a great friend and confidant and Bill Haden, Houston businessman and supporter who encouraged me to write this book. I thank you both.

To Sheriff Joe Arpaio of the Maricopa County, Arizona Sheriff's Office for his continuing endorsement and support of my efforts to bring conservative leadership to the Harris County Sheriff's Office. Every law enforcement leader in America should follow your lead and enforce the law.

A special thanks also to Linda Lutkus. Thank you for all of your help and friendship.

Thank You

Finally to every one of you who will read this book thank you for taking the time to follow my journey. I have been asked more times than I can tell you, "What's it like being a black Conservative Republican?" Well the answer is it is no different than being a Conservative Republican of any other race. It doesn't hurt, you don't have to take medication for it and it is the only proven way to bring our country out of the tailspin it is currently in. This nation means too much for us to allow it to fail.

Many believe that they cannot stand tall against adversity; it is not always important that you stand tall, but you must always find the strength to stand up!

Thank you all and may God bless you and the United States of America!

Carl Pittman

TABLE OF CONTENTS

Dedication to My Mother. xiii

Chapter 1   The Beginning. 23
Chapter 2   United States Marine Corps 44
Chapter 3   The Truth Distorted. 62
Chapter 4   Meeting a Payroll 69
Chapter 5   Enforcing the Law and Protecting Our Country. 74
Chapter 6   Black Leaders or Self-Appointed Black Leaders 83
Chapter 7   Entitlements 89
Chapter 8   Police Legitimacy and Accountability. 94
Chapter 9   Politics Mirrors Real Life – There are No
            Perfect People 98
Chapter 10 The U.S. Constitution and Our Founding
            Documents 101
Chapter 11 Government Over-Reach. 105
Chapter 12 Black vs. African American. 110
Chapter 13 TEA Party (Taxed Enough Already) 112
Chapter 14 The Conservative Voices .116
Chapter 15 Responsible Growth of the Grand Old Party 119
Chapter 16 The Attack. 126
Chapter 17 The Party of Lincoln and Reagan. 132
Chapter 18 Republican Women's Clubs (RWC). 134
Chapter 19 Primary vs. General Election Candidates 136
Chapter 20 Racism – Does it Exist in the GOP? 138

Chapter 21 Elected Officials 141
Chapter 22 The Media. 143
Chapter 23 The Value of Life. 148
Chapter 24 Bloggers 151
Chapter 25 Corruption in Government and Politics 154

Chapter 26 The Convenient Conservative 164
Chapter 27 How Republicans Win 174
Chapter 28 My Faith 176

Bibliography 181

TABLE OF ILLUSTRATIONS

Figure 1	Momma	xiii
Figure 2	Whites Only Cemetery	25
Figure 3	Hispanic Cemetery	26
Figure 4	Black Cemetery, where my mother and father are buried	26
Figure 5	The old house. It also leaned to the right!	33
Figure 6	Carl as a First Grader in 1969	34
Figure 7	Photo of my dad and grandfather, circa 1929	36
Figure 8	Emblem of the United States Marine Corps, the Eagle, Globe and Anchor	58
Figure 9	Sheriff Joe and Carl in Phoenix	75
Figure 10	Tent City Jail – Maricopa County, AZ	75
Figure 11	Illegal Alien Crossing Sign Warning in California (1980's)	81
Figure 12	Herman and Carl, 2011 Bay Area Republican Women Annual Dinner	100
Figure 13	Andrew Breitbart and Carl at Saddle-Up Texas Straw Poll – January 2012	115
Figure 14	An example of destructive and negative media which does not serve Republicans well	118

Everything we do should begin with

GOD

DEDICATION TO MY MOTHER

You are my hero and the bravest woman I have ever known. You taught me respect, compassion and discipline. You showed me that with hard work I could achieve anything to which I put my mind. You never gave up, and because of you, I will never give up. I remember everything you taught me and have tried always to make you proud. I love and miss you and look forward to seeing you again someday.

Figure 1 Momma

THE REPUBLICAN PARTY – A FAMILY DIVIDED

War is sometimes inevitable; and as Republicans we have spent far too much time fighting amongst ourselves. While engaged in this inner conflict our country has fallen deeper into the abyss of apathy, low expectations, and dependence on government rather than commitment to excellence, expectation of achievement, and fierce dedication to liberty. Our liberal enemies have us right where they want us, fighting each other instead of focusing on how we can solve our nation's problems and create more prosperity for all. Do you remember that phrase, "life, liberty and the pursuit of happiness"? As conservatives our highest priority must be to save this great republic, not to destroy each other. The current condition in which we find ourselves is a result of failed leadership by both Democrats and Republicans alike; there is more than enough blame to go around. I have always loved the story of our nation and how it was born. Do you think if we had it to do over today we could? I would like to believe that we could, but I really don't think so. There are too many self-described "patriots" that only have their own personal interest in mind. We must all remember that the decisions we make now will affect those generations to come. I don't want to ever have to sit and explain to my grandson why I did not do what was necessary to pass on his inheritance of freedom. – Carl Pittman

"Freedom is never more than one generation away from extinction. We didn't pass it to our children in the bloodstream. It must be fought for, protected, and handed on for them to do the same, or one day we will spend our sunset years telling our children and our children's children what it was once like in the United States where men were free." (Reagan 1967)– Ronald Reagan

COMMON SENSE CONSERVATISM

As a child I often heard people speak of "common sense" and almost every time I heard it someone would say, <u>but</u> "You know common sense isn't common!" In order to know where you are going, it's important to know where you are and where you've been. Late last year (2012) I went to see a movie entitled, "Lincoln" starring the actor Daniel Day Lewis. This movie was historically accurate and primarily focused on the facts that led to the passing of the 13th Amendment to the United States Constitution which abolished slavery. I would strongly suggest that all black Americans go and see this movie. It might just open some eyes as to the historical facts regarding the effort undertaken by President Lincoln to gain the support in Congress necessary to pass the amendment. Remember President Abraham Lincoln was a Republican and Jefferson Davis, the President of the Confederate States, was a Democrat and did everything in his power to win the Civil War and to have his Democratic operatives defeat the amendment to keep blacks enslaved.

Today many blacks (and others) believe that the federal government's role is to provide everything for them. In essence it is another form of slavery. Whether its housing, food, education or healthcare many blacks have become so dependent upon the government they cannot imagine separating themselves from the government "nipple". This same mentality existed after the Emancipation Proclamation in 1863. Many blacks could not imagine leaving the "safety" of the plantation and many chose to stay. This mentality carries many from the cradle to the grave in full crippling, atrophying dependence on the government.

To the poor, a tax increase is a non-issue because most are not paying taxes. The thought of someone making a million dollars a year or more paying more taxes is of no concern to someone making twenty thousand dollars a year. Perspective is often determined by position. The government under both Republican and Democratic control has always taken far too much from the people. The people have consistently allowed themselves to be taken advantage of by listening to those with specific agendas instead of doing their own homework and making their own decisions. Voters who allow their decisions to be made by special interest groups who have no concern about what is beneficial to the people have no one to blame but themselves.

There are and always will be poor people (Matthew 26:11), but people are poor for several reasons. First there are some people who are just plain lazy and don't want to work. For those individuals I say that's your choice and my choice is to give you nothing but advice; and that advice is to get off your lazy asses and get a job if you want somewhere to live or something to eat. Second there are people who aren't lazy but are willing to "abuse" the system to get ahead or something for nothing. It really makes me angry when I see someone living in a shack, driving a new Cadillac Escalade to the grocery store to shop with their food stamps that they don't deserve. There is no shame in being poor or needing help, but the operative word is **need**. Finally, there are people who are poor by no fault of their own and would work if they had work to do, and the health to do so. Those are the people that I am inspired to help; because if we help them get started they will finish it themselves. That's the beauty of this great nation, if you want to get ahead, you can!

We as Republicans must put our words into action. If we are truly the party of Lincoln, we must help those who <u>cannot</u> help themselves. We <u>must</u> defend those who <u>cannot</u> defend themselves. This is where I think we as Republicans can do ourselves a favor in rebranding ourselves in the area of outreach. Outreach should not simply be done to add more Republicans to the voting rolls, but instead because it is the right thing to do. If the Republican Party wants to have its ranks grow with minorities then the Party must understand that this can be accomplished without compromising our values, but minorities must be completely welcomed into the party. Not just as voters or volunteers, but as part of Party leadership and elected officials.

In the 2012 Presidential election President Obama and the Democratic political machine convinced a great number of minorities, seniors and others that Republican Presidential nominee Mitt Romney was planning to end Social Security, Medicare, Medicaid and virtually every social program that many seniors and minorities depend on for their daily existence. Can you imagine someone loudly advocating for your lifetime source of support to end? Would that make you angry and distrusting of that individual or group? Well that, in a nutshell is why so many minorities identify so closely with the Democratic Party and believe that the Conservative movement is anti-minority. The facts are not applicable to the Democratic Party. The only thing that is relevant is their continued dominance in attracting minorities to their ranks.

As a Texan I have often heard it said that the nation goes the way that Texas goes. As of the writing of this book every statewide elected office is held by a Republican. Harris County, Texas (Houston) is the most populated county in Texas and was won by Barack Obama in 2008 and 2012. The Hispanic population is swelling throughout the state and many of them are voting Democrat. This trend does not bode well for Texas to remain a red state and if we intend for Texas to remain red we had all better wake up and do a much better job of attracting Hispanics and other minorities into the Party.

The attraction of Hispanics should not mean that we are going to overlook the illegal alien problem for fear of angering Hispanics. This is a country of laws and I believe that the Hispanic population not only recognizes that, but is desirous of it. Many Mexicans fled Mexico because of the lawlessness and lack of respect for the rule of law. Those Republicans who believe we should turn a blind eye to illegal immigration should be run out of the Party. We need sensible immigration solutions, not sanctioned lawlessness!

Now the truth is, Romney had been a successful businessman, and he understood that for these programs to successfully continue they needed to be restructured. But so often **the truth isn't what matters**, it is the **perception** that counts. The Democrats are very afraid of the truth and spend a large amount of money, time, and effort creating the desired perception.

As Christian Conservatives we must help those who cannot help themselves, but in my opinion if your situation isn't reflected by the list below, you might want to start looking for a job real fast.

- Elderly & children without other means of support.
- Physically and mentally disabled without other means of support.
- Those temporarily unemployed by no fault of their own. We help them find work and provide **temporary** assistance. By the way, 99 weeks for unemployment isn't helping, it's an excuse for many to not look for work until their unemployment checks run out.

We must communicate this in every way at our disposal. We must not let a single opportunity go by and fail to communicate and demonstrate that we are not the Party of the uncaring. The very lineage of this Party is of a people who care for and will protect those who cannot help themselves. There is no question that my decision many years ago to become a United States Marine was tied to this very belief. Poor is not tied to black, white or brown. Poor is a circumstance that can change!

John Wayne is famous for saying, "Life is tough, tougher if you're stupid!" (J. a. Wayne, Sands of Iwo Jima 1949) We must quit playing on the level of the competition and play above them. If we believe in our cause and are committed to achieving it then I believe that we will succeed!

Chapter 1

THE BEGINNING

"If you find yourself riding through hell; don't stop, keep going." (Churchill, True Origin Unknown Winter 2009-2010) – Winston Churchill

Who could have known a few months after my birth that President John F. Kennedy would be assassinated in Dallas, Texas and his Vice-President, from Texas, Lyndon B. Johnson would be sworn in as the 36th President of the United States of America?

On Monday, August 5th, 1963 the United States of America signed the Nuclear Test Ban Treaty with the Soviet Union (USSR) and I was born in a tiny two room, tin roof house in Fulshear, Fort Bend County, Texas. There was no indoor plumbing, no air conditioning only a window fan and a wood burning stove for cooking and heat. There were no interior doors, only a curtain to separate the kitchen and the main room. The house was very old with wood floors that were partially resting on the ground and that little house leaned slightly from left to right. The outhouse behind the house was a humbling experience and you only went when you really needed to go, especially during those cold Texas winters. My birth was attended by a mid-wife; I never saw the inside of a hospital until I was 13. I was the youngest of five children from four fathers and am so very grateful that my mother chose life for all of us.

My oldest sister, Mary was raised by her grandparents in nearby Simonton, Texas and my brother, Keith was raised by an aunt in the San Francisco, California area. I was raised with my other two sisters, Lila and Helen, there in that little house in Fulshear. My mother, Mattie, had only completed third grade and at the age of 13 left home and was effectively on her own, working in the fields, cleaning house and whatever other odd jobs she could find to survive. Mama could not read, could barely write her name, and struggled for most of her fifty years on this earth, but always told us that being poor didn't mean you had to be a thief, because you could work, nor be dirty, because soap was cheap.

There was an old hand pumped well at a neighbor's home and we would carry buckets of water in to a galvanized foot tub and warm it on the wood stove to a boil. We would add the hot water with three buckets of cold into a larger galvanized tub for our baths. In the winter we would share the bath water. I was the "baby" so I always got to bathe first. My mother always made me feel special and always told me that she knew that God had special things for me to do.

Some of my fondest memories of my mother were of doing laundry with her. That galvanized tub and aluminum washing-board was all we had. We would wring the clothes by hand and hang them on the outdoor clothes line. Many of my clothes were hand-me-downs from other families, but I was very content and happy. I never felt safer than the time spent with my mother, because I knew she would let no one harm me.

Growing up in Fulshear, Texas was a wonderful experience. There were, however, some things that I just never understood. Fulshear was a German settlement town that was founded in the late 1800's by Churchill Fulshear; it was an agricultural town built around a railroad right-of-way. The population in the late 1960's and early 1970's was around 300. But strangely enough there were and are still today three (3) functioning and very segregated cemeteries. We may come from many walks of life and different socio-economic conditions, but there is a reason there are no luggage racks on a hearse. You can't take any of your earthly wealth with you – Death is the great equalizer.

Cemeteries in Fulshear, TX

Figure 2 Whites Only Cemetery

Figure 3 Hispanic Cemetery

Figure 4 Black Cemetery, where my mother and father are buried

My first experience with racism occurred at the age of five, in the summer of 1968. I was walking home with my sisters on a Saturday afternoon from Dozier's Market, a small country store in Fulshear famous for its BBQ. I had been annoying my older sister Lila for candy, as was the norm. The roads on our side of town were not paved and were covered with gravel. Passing vehicles would carry a dust cloud when they passed.

Most people would slow down so as not to cover those walking with dirt. I didn't understand what they were doing or why they were doing it, but suddenly my sisters grabbed and pulled me into the roadside ditch and huddled over me. I heard an approaching vehicle speeding our way on that gravel road, and as it passed, a glass bottle was thrown that landed at our feet as someone yelled, "Niggers!"

That was the first time in my life I had heard that word. I was five years old. I had no idea what it meant. All the way home, I kept asking, "What are niggers, what are niggers?" Neither of my sisters would answer as we ran towards home. I would come to find out that this was a most hurtful word meant only to cause pain.

This was not the last time I was to hear the word, and I became very aware of the destructive intent meant by many of those who have used it. The first and probably best definition I've ever heard for the word *"nigger"* was – "a low down, dirty person." So in my mind the person who threw that bottle at us fit the description, because that was a low down, dirty thing to do.

You may remember the 1995 Los Angeles, California, murder trial of former National Football League great O.J. Simpson. The defense team put the word *"nigger"* on trial when they called lead Los Angeles Police Department Detective Mark Fuhrman to the witness stand. Fuhrman's involvement as an investigator, holding key prosecution evidence, was damning and had to be dealt with by the defense. Now, before I go any further I have to say this: I believe the Simpson verdict was a perfect example of jury nullification. Jury nullification, in simple terms, means that regardless of what evidence is produced during trial, the verdict will not change. I lived in San

The Personal Journey of a Black Common Sense Conservative

Diego, California, at the time, and the O. J. Simpson trial was everywhere, all the time.

A just outcome was probably doomed from the start. A star-struck California Superior Court Judge, Lance Ito, was presiding. The prosecution team was led by Los Angeles County Assistant District Attorneys Marcia Clark and Christopher Darden. The defense "Dream Team" consisted of Johnny Cochran, Robert Shapiro and Robert Kardashian (yes, that would be the father of the Kardashian girls). Remember, "If the glove doesn't fit; you must acquit"? I recall watching as O. J. "struggled" to put on a glove that looked like a pretty good fit to me.

In my more than twenty years of law enforcement I have rarely seen a criminal trial lawyer ask a question for which they didn't already have the answer. On March 15, 1995 Los Angeles Police Department Homicide Detective Mark Fuhrman was cross examined by legendary defense attorney F. Lee Bailey and while under oath Fuhrman denied using the word "nigger" at any time in the previous ten years. (Abrahamson 1996)

Now I didn't personally know Mark Fuhrman, but as a law enforcement officer working in Southern California in the mid 80's and early 90's I knew it was highly unlikely that Mark Fuhrman had not used the word "nigger". I had heard the word used many times on the streets as a police officer, by citizens and police officers alike.

On August 29, 1995 the Fuhrman tapes were played in open court with the jury absent, and well let's just say Mark Fuhrman had "misremembered" using the "N" word. On October 3, 1995 O.J. Simpson was found not guilty of two counts of murder. I have often wondered just how much that event helped shape

The Beginning

the jury's verdict. There was, in my opinion, a serious case of jury nullification in play, but did the "N" word play a part?

The question is why did Mark Fuhrman lie? I believe Fuhrman lied because of the impact that the word "nigger" has in our society and he feared that if the truth were known to the jury it would damage his credibility and ultimately the prosecution's case. It is likely that the Simpson case was lost before opening statements because of the "star factor" and distrust of the police by some members of the jury. Fuhrman was absolutely correct in that assumption, but what should he have done?

Fuhrman should have told the truth, by telling that jury exactly what they already suspected. Fuhrman should have admitted to having used the word. The use of the word "nigger" did not prove that he had planted evidence and his ownership of it may have proven to the jury that he may have needed racial sensitivity training, but he wasn't a liar. The power of the "N" word had played a part in letting a probable murderer go free.

"It takes the black keys and the white keys both, to make perfect harmony." (Goodman 2013)–Benny Goodman

If the word "nigger" is truly offensive to black people, then blacks should not refer to one another as "niggers". How many popular music hits have been marketed and sold to white kids in the suburbs containing the word "nigger" or "nigga". I don't know about you, but I sometimes like to sing songs that have a catchy beat. Do you see the problem here? If little white Bobby from suburbia is riding the city bus and starts singing that song; well I think you can figure out what happens next. We will only move beyond racism when we **all** stop participating in it.

Racism is not genetic. It cannot be identified in our DNA sequence. It is a learned behavior. It is quite easy to fear what you do not understand. I am reminded of how I saw the U. S. Marine Corps deal with race. **There were no black marines or white marines. There were light green and dark green, but all Marines!** I would like to think that I am an intelligent man, and I have never found it in myself to hate anyone based upon their race. There are only two types of people; good ones and bad ones. If you are a good one then I like you. If you are a bad one, then I don't want much to do with you.

Life presents us with challenges. When there are no more challenges, you're dead. I stuttered as a young boy and from the age of five or so it frustrated me so that I would sometimes just cry. The thoughts were in my head, but I just couldn't get them out. My mother prayed for me and took me to more revivals than I can remember to have people "lay hands" on me. Well without any speech therapy I outgrew it and by the time I was eleven or so it had virtually disappeared. My sisters would sometimes tell me that I didn't talk much when I was young, and then later I wouldn't shut up. I believe that God heard all of those prayers and not only healed me, but gave me a peace and a knack for public speaking.

Hard work was a normal part of life and I enjoyed knowing that if I worked I could earn my own money. If I worked more I could earn more! At ten years old I had two yards that I cut every Saturday during the spring and summer. There were two elderly sisters that lived together and had a small yard, (they always told me how cute I was) and they paid me $12.00 to cut their yard every Saturday. Ms. Beulah had a much larger yard, but would only pay me $10.00. Ms. Beulah always encouraged

The Beginning

me to work hard and earn my own way so as to never have to depend on someone else's money. I must have been a sight, pulling that little red mower and gas can around Fulshear. That was almost $100 dollars a month in 1973 for a ten year old. I would spend no more than five dollars a week and would save the rest. I had already learned as a ten year old what most Democrats never learn and that was, saving money is a good thing. Working always made me feel like I belonged; I never wanted anyone to give me anything except an opportunity.

My mother was my hero and watching her work to take care of us was such an inspiring thing. Mama could pick three to four hundred pounds of pecans in a day. We picked pecans and cotton to get by. When I hear people complain about their station in life I just want to tell them to work more and complain less! My mother was a very large woman until she was diagnosed with diabetes in 1973. She was one of the most disciplined people I had ever seen; when the doctor told her she had to lose weight she did just that. She slimmed down to just a fraction of herself. She would always tell us kids, "Don't let your mouth kill you".

We ate more baked chicken, fish and green beans than you can imagine. To this very day I am not very fond of fish because we ate a lot of it because it was free to catch and someone was always giving it away. I was eight years old when I decided to peek into a pot on the stove. I pushed back the lid and suddenly I came face to face with a set of eyes looking back at me. It was a pot of fish head soup and it nearly scared me to death. That taught me a lesson about peeking into pots on the stove!

Mama never complained and I knew that she would do anything in the world for us and nobody could mess with us, her babies. Mama's constant prayer was to live long enough to see all of her children to adulthood.

My mother gave birth to five children, of which I was the youngest. The five of us children were fathered by four different men and my mother never married. This surely isn't the preferred method, but I am proud that she made the decision for life in a time and under circumstances when many would not.

My father, Frederick Douglas Davis, was born in 1912 and was much older than my mother who was 23 years his junior. He served in the U.S. Army before I was born and I didn't get to know him well because he died in 1970 when I was in first grade. My mother always told me how much she loved him, but because he was not the father of my sisters, Helen and Lila, she would not marry him because she didn't want to bring a man into a house with her little girls. I didn't understand it then, but I came to appreciate that mama placed the safety of her children above everything, even herself.

After the death of my father, his cousin took me under his wing and was a great role model for me. His name was Dexter Martin; he owned quite a bit of land adjacent to the Brazos River in Fort Bend County, Texas. He was the first black business man I had ever known. I called him Mr. Dexter and I spent a great deal of time with him between the age of six and thirteen years of age. He taught me the pecan business during my early years. Mr. Dexter was a deacon in his church and kept the church cemetery.

One Saturday afternoon he and I were in the cemetery mowing and tending the grounds and after we were done he asked me to take a look at the grave stones and asked me if I noticed anything special about them. I studied them for a few moments without understanding what he wanted me to notice. Do you notice the names are the largest writings on them? That's because your name is the most important thing you have and the only thing you can take with you when you go. He stressed to me the importance of keeping your word and protecting your name. I would be reminded of this many times during my 2012 race for Harris County Sheriff.

Figure 5 The old house. It also leaned to the right!

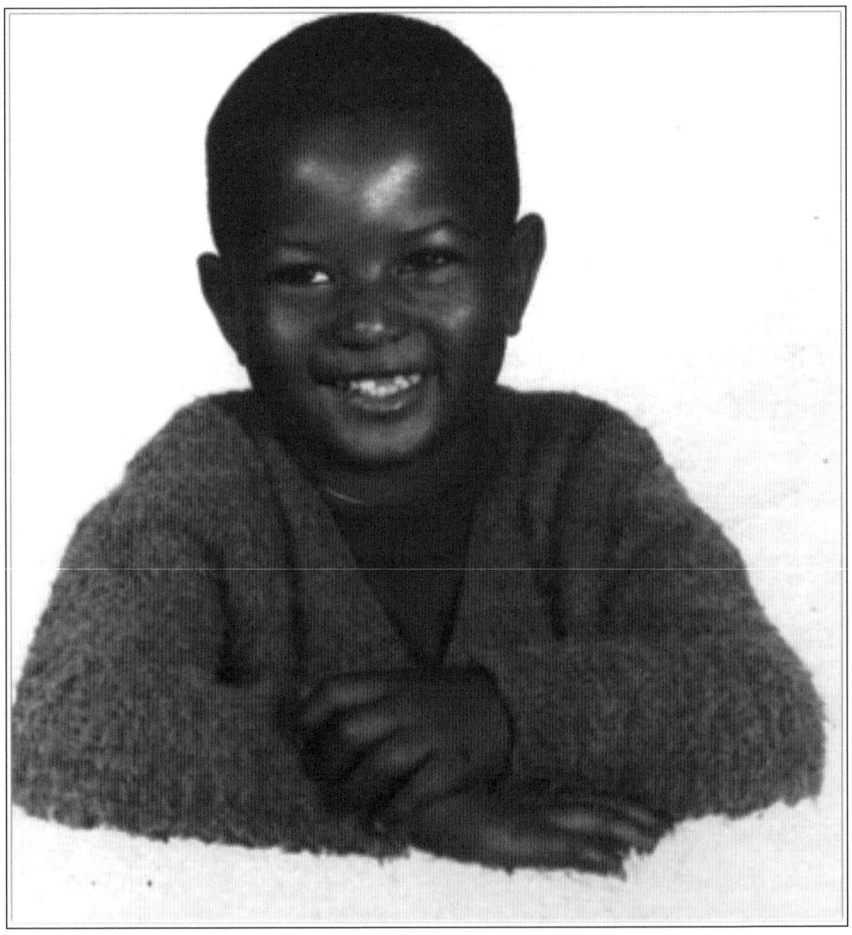

Figure 6 Carl as a First Grader in 1969

Mama's Babies

In 1975 my mother proved that it was not wise to mess with her baby. The Baptist church was putting on a community program that included a play. I was cast to have a leading role at 11 years old. An older boy, about 16, Jackie, decided he wanted the role and decided to try and pick a fight with me. It scared me more than anything so after finishing rehearsal at church I came home feeling a little down.

The Beginning

My mother asked me what was wrong and I explained to her what happened. I will never forget her picking up that old black rotary dial phone and dialing Jackie's aunt. In the calmest voice Mama said, **"Viola, this is Mattie. If you want to keep Jackie in the land of the living you tell him to leave Carl alone."** I can tell you that Jackie never bothered me again; in fact Jackie went on to become the pastor of that church and remains as pastor today.

My maternal grandmother, Mandy, was a tall, slim, dark woman. She was a very quiet and superstitious woman who believed very strongly in the spirit world and she passed this on to my mother. My maternal grandfather, Adolph, died before I was born, but had worked for the Imperial Sugar Company in Sugar Land, Texas for many years. My paternal grandmother, Lillie Ellis Davis, was an educated woman who had been an educator in the Galveston area. In her later years she would live and eventually die while in San Francisco, California, living with my dad's sister, my Aunt Ruby Jewel. My paternal grandfather was of Spanish descent and passed before my birth.

The constant admonition made to me by my mother was "**If you ever have children, they eat even if you don't**". How different this is from what we see today! Mama believed that discipline was the cornerstone of good order. <u>Mama always told us that she whipped us so the police would never have to do so.</u> Well as in most things mama was right, and none of us ever saw the inside of a jail cell.

Figure 7 Photo of my dad and grandfather, circa 1929

The Great Fire

In the summer of 1969 I turned six years old. As most little country boys at the time I always carried a few wooden matches in my pocket. I have no idea why; it's not as though I needed them for anything, but at the time it was cool. My sisters and I had been playing at a neighbor girl's house. Renee had the best backyard for hide-and-go-seek, with big trees and plenty of old sheds and barns to hide in and around. Renee was about five years older than me and was the best of friends with my sister, Helen.

Whenever we played together the girls, especially Renee, would tease me because she was always getting new toys and didn't want me to play with them. On this particular Saturday afternoon Renee was playing with a new doll and wouldn't let me play with it. She teased and teased me. Well soon enough her grandmother told all of us kids that we needed to go home so Renee could eat lunch and take a nap. Renee left her new doll on the front porch and I decided that I would hide it to get back at her for teasing me. Well I got the doll and went around to the side of their house. I remembered that I had some matches in my pocket; so I thought it would be funny to burn the dolls long hair off and leave it on the porch. Well let's just say that was the worst mistake I had made up to that point in my young five years of life. I quickly discovered that doll was made from 100% petroleum products. As soon as the flames touched the doll's hair it literally exploded into flames and I panicked, and threw it away, and it landed in the garage. I was so afraid, that all I could think to do was to run home as fast as possible.

I got home and in hindsight made another critical error. I asked my mother if I could take a bath. Now that must have sounded like a strange request from a five year old boy on a sunny summer Saturday afternoon. I brought in the galvanized tub and the water from the pump was warm enough that I didn't need to warm it. Take it from me it was soon about to be as warm as it had ever been. Just as I was calming down I heard in the distance the wail of the old community volunteer fire truck just as I heard my mother announce to herself, "What is all that smoke coming from?"

Suddenly she was standing over me and asked, "Boy, what did you do?" I was too afraid to speak and she told me to get out of the bath and get dressed. I began to cry as I explained to her what I had done and she said to me, "Don't tell me, save it!" Mama marched me down the road and by that time most of Fulshear had arrived on the scene and the barn was fully engulfed in flames. I could see Renee's grandmother, who I always called Miss Lillie, pacing back and forth on the road in front of their house seeming puzzled as to what had caused the fire. Now unfortunately, today many parents would have kept the secret with their child, but not my mother. Mama told me that I had to go and tell Miss Lillie what I had done. I could not believe what she wanted me to do! Was there no mother–son loyalty? Not a bit, not that day!

I begged my mother to not make me tell, but she gave me the "look" and I knew that I had better get going. I can remember thinking while I was walking towards Miss Lillie that one day this would all be funny. I finally got my little legs to get me to Miss Lillie and tugged at her housedress, but she told me to go away. Well I had tried right? I looked back at my mother

The Beginning

hoping that she had changed her mind about what I had to do and well, let's say she had not. I was finally able to get Miss Lillie's attention and told her what I had done. I can honestly tell you that what happened next was turned out to be the most painful day of my life.

Miss Lillie told me to go around to the other side of the house and bring her an old bridle strap that was hanging on a nail. I was in no particular rush to get to it and when I returned she whipped me in front of the entire town and my mother watched. I was hit everywhere except for the bottom of my feet and there was plenty of encouragement from the crowd to give me more. She whipped me for what felt like forever and when she was done my mother took the bridle strap from her and whipped me again. I thought for sure those two women were going to kill me. To make matters worse my mother whipped me again that evening before I went to bed. I was so afraid of fire after that day, I didn't even want to eat hot food for a while, but I learned an important lesson and that was to never play with fire again.

I am not in any way suggesting that parents today administer this kind of discipline on their children because you would go to jail and CPS would most likely remove your children from your home. This story is told just to explain the thought process in the late 1960's of how parents could, if they chose, discipline their children. Oh, and by the way I still haven't found this experience too funny even after all these years. My children got a kick out of the story; they never met their grandmother as she passed before they were born.

My mother believed in not sparing the rod. I remember that there were times when mama would have to leave us alone and in order to make sure we would act right while she was gone she would call us in and "Give us a taste". That's right, she would whip us just a little to make sure that we knew that if we got out of line while she was gone we would get the rest when she got home, and believe me you did not want the rest. Where was due process?

Earlier I wrote of not seeing the inside of a hospital until I was thirteen. On New Year's Day 1977 I was at home watching television. My mother and sisters were at a neighbor's house and there were people everywhere. It was a brisk, sunny day and my mother phoned home and told me it was too nice a day to be in the house and to turn off the television and come outside. Well I did exactly what Mama said and went outside. Some of the neighborhood guys were just getting ready to start a football game and asked me if I wanted to play. Well of course I did, as I loved football and had gotten a new pair of cleats for Christmas and this was my first opportunity to try them out.

I was playing running back and while running a sweep play as the ball carrier, I decided to cut back. I stepped on a plastic cheese wrapper; you know the kind that contains a slice of American cheese. My foot went out from under me and as I was falling to the ground I attempted to break my fall with my left hand and "snap". I fell to the ground and felt excruciating pain. I had broken my left wrist and the bone was exposed. It swelled immediately and someone notified my mother.

My mother arrived and I was doing everything I could think of to calm her down. There was blood everywhere and all I could think of was that I didn't want my mother to be afraid. There was no 911 system so the call was placed to the Fort

The Beginning

Bend County Sheriff's Office and they dispatched an ambulance out to Fulshear from Richmond. It was almost an hour from the time of the accident until the ambulance arrived. I remembered them placing an inflatable air cast on my left arm and loading me onto a gurney.

They placed me in the ambulance and my mother never left my side. The ride from Fulshear to Polly Ryan Hospital in Richmond was 25 minutes. The gurney was covered with my blood and I was feeling drowsy. The last thing I remembered was a nurse asking if I had ever received a tetanus shot. I don't remember what the answer was because by that time I was out. The date was Saturday, January 1, 1977.

My next memory was waking up in Hermann Hospital on Hwy 59 near Houston and the date was Saturday, January 8, 1977. My mother was sitting next to my bed and holding my right hand. My left arm was in a cast from just below my shoulder and it encompassed my left hand to immobilize my wrist. I later found that I had been given an injection of penicillin and unknown to anyone at the time, I was allergic to penicillin. I had been in a coma like state for more than eight days. I remembered telling my mother that I had been afraid that I was going to die when she told me something that I've never forgotten. She asked me if I wanted to go to heaven and I told her yes. She then told me that as long as my soul was good with God to not to be afraid to die.

Faith carried us through the toughest of times. During times of severe weather we would always gather in that old house with the family bible and together recite the 23rd Psalm, "The Lord's Prayer". The Lord answered every one of those prayers and that little house stood strong.

I can remember many tropical storms and hurricanes coming out of the gulf, but I always felt that little house could stand against anything because we prayed together. Mama took us to church; she did not send us to church. Faith and family sustained us through those hard times and having a strong relationship with God has sustained me throughout the most difficult times in my life.

My mother offered advice on a number of things including lies. **"Don't ever get too angry when someone lies on you, because Jesus was lied on. So unless you are above Jesus; move on."** I found that advice during my 2012 run Harris County Sheriff to be quite helpful.

I can identify the first time that I recognized "fear" and that was the day my father was buried. I remember standing in the cemetery on a cold windy day and as I watched his casket lowered into the ground it hit me. What will happen to me now if mama dies? What would happen to all of us? Where would we live? I was terrified and I asked God to let me grow up fast so I could take care of and comfort my mother before she died.

Mama endured some very difficult times, but instilled in me a belief that God was in control and we always prayed that his will be done. One of her constant sayings was "Right is right and wrong is wrong, no matter who's doing it." I could not have imagined how much that quote would mold and lead me in the right direction. My mother would leave the house sometimes hours before we would all leave to wait for the school bus. She would start walking to make it to her house cleaning jobs that were about ten miles from Fulshear. I would sit on the right side of the school bus and watch for her as we rode the 17 miles from Fulshear to Rosenberg. I can remember so many

The Beginning

times seeing mama with her head held high as my school bus would pass her along FM 1093 and I would silently cry because there was nothing I felt I could do for her. I saw in my mother someone who did not complain about her station in life, but worked hard to take care of her responsibilities. If promoted today, those traits alone would substantially change the condition of our country.

I committed myself to being a good student, a good person and prayed to God that he would have mercy on my mother and let me someday be able to take good care of her for all she had done for us. Mama's constant prayer however was for God to let her live long enough to see all of her children to adulthood. My constant prayer to God was to let Mama live forever. God answered her prayers; at 50 years of age mama died on the night of August 16, 1985. I was two weeks past my 22nd birthday. I was just three weeks out of the United States Marine Corps and a cadet in the 103rd San Diego Regional Police Academy. Her death forever changed my life, but I remembered that God was in control and His will would be done. As many children believe that their mother was the best mother in the world, I just know that Mama was the best mother in the world for me. With my mothers' death, the only way I could repay her was to honor her request and to be a good man and honor my promises made to her. Her teachings and those requests have remained my constant guide throughout life and when I next see her I hope that she will agree that I have done so.

I had unknowingly been trained for the next stage in my life, becoming a United States Marine!

Chapter 2

UNITED STATES MARINE CORPS

"All that is necessary for evil to triumph is for good men to do nothing." (Burke 2010) – Sir Edmund Burke

I had been perfectly prepared for the Marines by a mother who knew that discipline was the cornerstone to good order. As a high school Junior in 1979 during a career day I saw a U.S. Marine on campus. Now if you have never seen a Marine in a dress uniform, please put that on your bucket list. There is nothing more "squared away" than that. I just knew that I wanted to be a part of that organization, so a few months later I took the oath and joined the United States Marine Corps under the "Delayed Entry Program". I had committed to joining the finest fighting force the world has ever known. Earning the title of United States Marine was truly special; it could not be bought, given, or stolen; it could only be earned through blood, sweat, and sometimes tears. I came to love and respect the Corps because of many things; but most of all, the principle that one's success was based upon their hard work, not their family name or political connections.

Have you ever wondered why certain individuals are appointed to key positions within the government when there are others more qualified? It happens at every level of government, from U.S. Ambassadors to Federal and State Judges, County Judges, County Commissioners and many others. The family name is more important than the skills or integrity to carry out the duties of the office. Many of our problems in this country exist because we have an abundance of individuals in office that want the power and prestige of the office, but don't want to uphold the responsibility of doing their duty. We need people with backbone and courage, not rhetoric and a politically connected last name. We don't need what I call "sheeple" **(people who follow blindly like a herd of sheep**.) We need leaders who will do what is right ahead of what is popular. We must have the courage to remove the bureaucracy in government by removing the unelected czars who have been elected by no one, but who continue to put their interests above ours. We must stop electing people that look good, sound good but are NO GOOD!

During my 2012 run for Sheriff in Harris County (Houston) Texas I apparently ruffled some feathers when I proposed the outrageous idea of enforcing and following the law. I even had the audacity to state that I would arrest public officials who broke the law. Don't you think that your county Sheriff ought to follow and enforce the law evenly? I had been endorsed by Sheriff Joe Arpaio of Maricopa County, Arizona and he agreed to come to Houston in support of my campaign in June of 2011. I had publicly stated that I would work to remove Harris County and the City of Houston from the Sanctuary Cities List. Sanctuary cities were identified as cities that had policies friendly to illegal aliens and turned a blind eye to their illegal presence. I believe that our country is under attack by the non-stop flood of illegals. This is one area that cannot be solely blamed on Democrats, because we have Republicans who are willing to sell this nation's safety and security for profit.

Now back to my race for Sheriff. The attacks came from Republicans and Democrats alike. I was warned by a local Republican that I would never get a penny of support from him and his associates if I followed through with Sheriff Arpaio coming to town. Are you surprised that these men decided to back my run-off opponent? I still have the threatening e-mails in which he tried to bully me from my position on illegal aliens. News flash–my beliefs and values are not for sale!

I even managed to upset a high ranking elected republican county official with the Arpaio visit because he had consistently stated around town that the Party should not even mount a challenger against the sitting Hispanic Democrat Sheriff because he had been the top vote getter in 2008.

That same high ranking elected republican county official had even gone so far as to propose this to the then County Republican Party Chair. Was this the twilight zone? Isn't the very purpose of the Republican Party to elect REPUBLICANS? I was even contacted by a local immigration attorney who was a self-proclaimed Republican, but she used a more subtle approach. She told me that she and some of her associates saw me as a fresh voice and a new minority face for the Party.

Now I've been around a while and knew the proverbial, "**but**" was coming. She went on to say, **but**, if you have "that man" (Arpaio, she wouldn't even say his name) come to town we will not support you. When she saw that approach wasn't working she changed tactics and inquired as to how much money I thought the campaign would cost. I did not have an accurate idea at the time, but figured I couldn't go wrong and threw out the figure of $500,000.00.

There was a pause, and she went on to tell me that she knew people who could help with those kinds of funds. I told her that I appreciated the offer, but my beliefs and principles were not for sale. I couldn't believe that I was being offered money as one of several Republican primary candidates more than a year before the primary, to keep Sheriff Joe Arpaio from coming to Houston.

I knew I had passed the test: I stuck to my principles and knew that I would not change because I was right. By the way Sheriff Joe Arpaio came to Houston on Friday June 3, 2011 and it was a full weekend with us both appearing live with Michael Berry a local conservative radio talk show host that afternoon, where Sheriff Arpaio again endorsed me live on the air. The weekend culminated with a large rally fundraiser in Humble, Texas billed as "A Gathering of Patriots". One thing for sure; June 4, 2011 had to be the hottest day of the year and our event was an outdoor covered event. Sheriff Arpaio was an absolute hit and he and I keep in touch to this day.

Sheriff Joe Arpaio is one of the most decent men and law enforcement leaders I have ever known. If every Sheriff in America ran their office in a similar fashion we would live in a very different country. We would also live in safer communities, but who's worried about that, right?

Your constitutionally elected Sheriff is the highest elected law enforcement official in their respective county and they have a sworn duty to protect the constitution. No one is exempt from the enforcement of the law and that includes federal officers. One self-described "blogger" attacked me for stating that as sheriff I would remove federal agents from the county if they violated the law in my county. The real question is why wouldn't he want them removed?

The people should not live in fear of their elected government; if anything the elected should fear the people. The government is here to serve us! Thomas Jefferson summed it up this way: "When the people fear the government there is tyranny, when the government fears the people there is liberty."

It was my first run at public office and I felt like a rookie police officer. I was running to actually do the job of the elected Sheriff of a county and knew that I could make a difference. I had proposed a zero-based budget policy to locate and cut waste. During a candidate debate one of my primary opponents stated that zero-based budgeting was tried under President Carter's administration and it didn't work. My response was that shouldn't have been a surprise since nothing worked well under Jimmy Carter's administration. I was actually going to enforce the law against anyone who broke it including elected officials. I think I made some people nervous and they showed it by their frequent attacks. That's okay because I am far from done. If they haven't yet figured it out, Marines don't quit!

The Harris County Sheriff's office is the largest Sheriff's office in Texas and the third largest Sheriff's office in the United States, behind Los Angeles County California and Cook County (Chicago) Illinois Sheriff's office. In 2012 we were operating on approximately a $397,000,000.00 budget with out of control spending. Can you believe the Democrat in office in 2009 decided it was a great business decision to spend approximately $400,000.00 on a SWAT command vehicle and the agency didn't even have a SWAT team? During the fiscal cuts of 2011 and 2012 budget years the sheriff's office budget was the only county agency budget that was not cut and in fact received a 4% budget increase. With a population of nearly 4.2 million residents in Harris County, Texas the agency needed a fiscally conservative, militarily disciplined, veteran law enforcement and businessman at the helm. I believe that I was the perfect fit for the office and that fact scared some of the entrenched local politicians who wanted things to remain the same, even if it meant keeping the incumbent, overspending Democrat in office

The founding fathers knew that America would be safest by not establishing a monarchy. The twenty-second Amendment of the United States Constitution set a term limit for election to the office of President of the United States. The U. S. Congress passed the amendment on March 21, 1947 and established that no person shall be elected to the office of the President more than twice, and no person who has held the office of President, or acted as President, for more than two years of a term to which some other person was elected President shall be elected to the office of President more than once.

The Military Oath of Enlistment:
I, (Insert name), do solemnly swear that I will support and defend the Constitution of the United States against all enemies foreign and domestic; that I will bear true faith and allegiance to the same; and that I will obey the orders of the President of the United States and the orders of the officers appointed over me, according to the regulations

of the Uniform Code of Military Justice. So help me God. (U.S. Army Center of Military History 1960)

The taking of the oath for me was a sacred event. This same oath had been taken and sworn to by all Marines who came before including those who had given the ultimate sacrifice to protect this great nation. I have never forgotten what this meant to me and please be sure to note: **there is no expiration date and this oath is alive within me for as long as I draw breath!**

Early morning on July 27, 1981 an olive drab green Marine Corps van arrived to pick me up from my house in Fulshear, Texas. I hugged Mama and told her not to worry, but I knew that she would because so many of the young men of her generation had gone to Vietnam and never came home. My sisters Helen and Lila were excited and it took every bit of strength I had not to cry because I hated leaving my mother, but I knew if I was to have a chance to take care of her I needed to leave because there were no opportunities there in Fulshear.

We drove into downtown Houston to the processing center and then to a local hotel with a meal voucher for the last night before boot camp.

I awoke at 0500 hours on the morning of July 28, 1981. There were several recruits headed for San Diego to Marine Corps Recruit Depot (MCRD). I was selected to carry the orders for the group of Marine Recruits leaving from Houston; there were seven of us. We were driven to Intercontinental Airport in north Houston at approximately one o'clock for a six o'clock flight to the west coast. The flight was uneventful and I will never forget how beautiful San Diego, California is from the air as you are on final approach into San Diego's Lindberg Field.

Coronado Bay Bridge, to the left side of the aircraft, and the view of San Diego Bay was spectacular. Final approach takes you just north of downtown; you can literally see the inside of the office buildings as the aircraft quickly drops over Interstate 5 and onto the runway. This was definitely not Fulshear, Texas and I remembered to look out the right side of the aircraft because this was the southern fence of Marine Corps Recruit Depot, my new home for the next several months. I thought to myself; this can't be too bad – this place is beautiful! Did I have another thing coming! We exited the aircraft via an exterior ladder and walked across the tarmac to the terminal. I saw the "Military Desk" and did a quick head count to make sure that none of our group of seven had changed their mind.

All present and accounted for so I walked to the "Military Desk" and gave our orders to the Marine representative. We were instructed to exit the terminal and to load onto the green bus and wait. We waited for what seemed like hours as other recruits were arriving from other parts of the country. Darkness fell, and just as we were wondering if we were going to spend the night onboard the bus; a tall, thin perfectly groomed Marine stepped onto the bus. His campaign cover (hat for all you non-military types.) tilted forward to cover his eyes; he said, "When I call your name answer up!" He began to call last name, first name, until we all answered and another man stepped onto the bus and sat in the driver's seat. We quickly continued small talk amongst ourselves as we seemed to drive forever just to get to the other side of the fence from the airport.

The bus slowed and rounded a corner and then there was nothing but bright lights. The main gate to MCRD-San Diego was manned by a Marine Military Police Officer who snapped to attention and waved us through. The bus continued forward for a few moments and then stopped in front of a Quonset hut. The Quonset huts are the metal buildings that resemble a large aluminum drain pipe cut in half. There were dozens of Marine D.I.s (Drill Instructors) and the situation quickly turned serious. Now mind you, I was fresh out of high school football and track. I was 6'-02", 175 and confident, but I must admit, I was a bit concerned.

A Marine D.I. stepped on the bus and he looked as though he had been forged from solid steel. He was probably 6'-4" and 200 pounds and his campaign cover was nearly touching the ceiling of the bus. He spoke in a voice that sounded almost mechanized, he did not blink and he didn't even appear to breath.

To this day I am not exactly sure of what he said next, but I knew for sure he was very much in charge and he was absolutely serious. Now remember everything done in boot camp is done "quickly". We raced off of the bus and into the Quonset hut where we grabbed a plastic tub, an adjustable green utility web belt, canteen holder, and canteen and poncho liner. We then raced back outside onto a large parade deck covered with yellow foot prints. We were pushed and pulled onto the footprints that formed a perfect formation in front of a large earth toned colored stucco building with only one door with a single light above the doorway.

The D.I.s all simultaneously went nuts, they thought we were all deaf so they screamed and the exercise apparently could only be properly carried out when the campaign covers were ramming into your forehead as the verbal and sometimes physical abuse continued. Face to face and six inches was apparently the desired proximity for verbal communication. Spit was flying and some of the recruits were surely wondering if they had gotten on the wrong bus. **This is the proper time to tell you that we would live in a very different and better country if every American male, at the very least, went to Marine Corps boot camp.**

The D.I.s were swarming everywhere, yelling, pushing and constantly reminding us that mommy and daddy could not help us. If you would like to see a near perfect glimpse into Marine Corps boot camp life, try and find a copy of the movie, Full Metal Jacket. Many were just coming to the realization that they had not been told the whole story by their Marine recruiters. We were all told that our girlfriends and or wives (which were all suddenly named Mary Jane Rotten-Crotch) were fornicating with some guy named "Jody" at that very moment. I would later come to understand that this entire process, right down to the night time arrival, was designed to disorient new recruits. It was approximately 9:00 pm and there were approximately 200 new recruits present from all over the country.

We were told that we were about to begin our transformations from civilians into Marines. This meant "haircuts" and there were no style choices; we were only told if we had a mole on our heads to put a finger on it. By the time I entered the barber shop it was nearly ankle deep in hair, cut by five or six barbers, and they were stripping us to the scalp. The process was very cold and impersonal. I even saw a couple recruits with tears in their eyes. I didn't see them after that night, **but I heard they quit and joined the Navy.** There was definitely no crying in the Marine Corps.

We then were herded into another room where we were given large paper bags. We were told to remove all clothing. So here I am standing naked in a room with a couple hundred strangers with what was left of my afro on the floor in the next room. We were only allowed to keep one religious medallion or a cross, address book and shoes. All other clothing and property was placed into the paper bags and labeled with our names and training cycle numbers. We would not see these bags again until graduation.

This process continued on into the night and early morning. We were issued our first issue of t-shirts, socks, boxer underwear, toilet kit and camouflage utilities.

After a personal screening to see if anyone was stupid enough to bring pornography or drugs into Marine Corps boot camp and to make sure no one had turned suicidal, we were then herded into a large squad bay with around a hundred of the oldest metal bunk beds you could imagine. We were then ordered to "quickly" execute the three "S". Shit, shower and shave. Now I understood the first two, but I had never had a razor on my baby face in my life, but that didn't matter. This was pure chaos. Two hundred recruits in a head (the military term for bathroom) designed for twenty-five and most of us had never shaved before. It looked like a "B-grade" horror movie; there was blood everywhere.

What a site! White t-shirt, white boxers, virtually bald and bleeding from the multiple razor cuts to my formerly baby face; this was a far cry from the poster of the Marine in dress blues I had envisioned. We scrambled into our racks after a fire watch (sentry) was selected and by then it was around 3:00 AM. Fire watch was the duty that every Marine has pulled, keeping watch for danger while other marines rested, but we weren't even marines yet.

I'm not sure that I ever fell asleep that first night, but reveille came at 0500 hrs. Again the D.I.s came in throwing aluminum trash cans and lids everywhere. We were disoriented, tired, hungry and yes, a bit nervous. Most of us had not eaten a meal since we left our point of departure more than 24 hours earlier. We were rushed to–you guessed it, the three "S" again. More blood and guts for the Corps. We were herded out onto the parade deck and waited for about three hours to be picked up and marched to our temporary barracks where recruits were held until enough recruits had arrived to start a new training cycle.

Marine Corps boot camp is a rite of passage. It cannot be purchased or given; it must be earned. From that first night's arrival to the countless hours in the sand pit or on the "grinder" learning to drill, learning how to handle your weapon, studying and learning Marine Corps history and those legendary figures such as Chesty Puller (the only Marine to be award the Navy Cross five times). (Belew n.d.) Learning hand to hand combat and hours on the rifle range learning to reach out and touch someone without them ever knowing you were there. Laying in your rack at night at full attention with your rifle and singing the Marine Corps Hymn.

I celebrated my 18th birthday in boot camp and I can only tell you that there is no birthday party quite like a United States Marine Corps boot camp sponsored party. I will never forget the concern I had that night during mail call. There I sat in the squad bay sitting on the deck wearing a white tee shirt, white boxers and shower shoes along with the rest of my platoon.

I had been in boot camp for two weeks and it was August 5, 1981. I saw a small cardboard box sitting on the deck near the duty drill instructor and hoped that it was not a birthday gift. Well as mail was distributed I had that sinking feeling that the box was for me, and then it happened.

PITTMAN! My heart raced as I quickly rose from the deck and moved quickly to the front and stood at attention as I barked out. "Sir, Private Pittman reporting for mail call as ordered, Sir! I could see that the box was addressed to me and my sisters had drawn hearts and kisses on the box. The D.I. expressed to me in no uncertain terms that since it was my birthday it would only be right to have a party. I was ordered to open the package and then hand the opened package to the D.I. (Federal regulations prohibited them from opening recruit mail.) From inside the box he removed two packages of Chips Ahoy cookies, one package of Nutter Butters and one package of Pecan Sandies.

Well I will tell you again that you have never had a birthday party until you have one thrown for you in Marine Corps boot camp. My platoon gathered around and they actually were allowed to sing "Happy Birthday" to me. Then the celebration began, with me alone in the pushup position; I was the entertainment. Now if you have never heard of a Chinese pushup here is a brief description: Stand flat footed on the floor and bend over at the waist placing your palms flat on the deck. Step #1- Lower your upper body to the deck until your head touches. Step #2- Return to starting position and ………Repeat!!!!

Now if you don't want to take my word for it that these are devastatingly difficult. Go to your doctor and get medical clearance before you try them. I can only tell you that I spent approximately 45 minutes doing those damn things. The next morning my triceps and biceps had swelled to the point that I could not get my camouflage top to fit over them. I think my drill instructor was a little concerned that I would ask to go to sick call, but I didn't. After three days of fire watch the swelling went down and I was functional enough to get back to training. The result was huge arms because I had completely destroyed the muscles. The lesson here for me was that Marines don't quit; tired and hurting is no excuse to stop. Pain is simply weakness leaving the body and we will get all the rest we need when we're dead.

I don't mean to brag, but there is nothing in this world more committed than a dedicated Marine. We have covered the globe and winning is the only thing we know. This is the true meaning of "American Exceptionalism". In contrast to some current politicians, we never apologize for leadership or for being the best. We are at our best when we are strong. There's not a Marine I know who wouldn't rather die on their feet than live on their knees.

Can you tell by the Marine Corps hymn what we've done and who we are?

From the Halls of Montezuma
To the shores of Tripoli;
We fight our country's battles
In the air, on land and sea;
First to fight for right and freedom
And to keep our honor clean;
We are proud to claim the title
Of United States Marine

**Our flag's unfurled to every breeze
From dawn to setting sun;
We have fought in every clime and place
Where we could take a gun;
In the snow of far-off Northern lands
And in sunny tropic scenes;
You will find us always on the job
The United States Marines**

**Here's health to you and to our Corps
Which we are proud to serve;
In many a strife we've fought for life
And never lost our nerve;
If the Army and the Navy-ever look on Heaven's scenes;
They will find the streets are guarded
By United States Marines!**

The other branches of the U.S. Military often find themselves trying to understand the confidence of a Marine. Simply put we are the finest fighting force the world has ever known. Even our emblem the eagle, globe and anchor were assembled in a most impressive manner.

Figure 8 Emblem of the United States Marine Corps, the Eagle, Globe, and Anchor

We took the eagle from the Air Force.
We borrowed a rope from the Army.
We stole the Anchor from the Navy.
On the seventh day while God rested, we overran his perimeter and took the Globe.
And we've been running the whole show since.

Now that ought to tell you a thing or two about the Marine Corps!

Military Occupational Specialty (MOS) 0311 – "Combat Infantry Marine" our life was in the field. I have a great deal of respect for anyone who has served this country, whether as a member of the Army, Navy or Air Force, but I am not shy to tell you that no enemy on the planet wants to have to deal with a hard charging, dedicated United States Marine. I was assigned to the 3rd Battalion, 5th Marines of the 1st Marine Division. The structure and discipline of the Marine Corps was a perfect fit for me. I enjoyed knowing that I was part of an organization with such a great history and reputation around the world.

This was never more evident to me than in December of 1984 on Christmas Eve when I returned home on holiday leave. I flew into Houston's Intercontinental Airport from San Diego and a childhood friend was running late picking me up from the airport. I was wearing my "dress blues" and as a Marine Corporal my blues had the famous "blood stripe" down the pant seams. I found myself surrounded in the terminal by other travelers offering handshakes, thanking me for my service and offering to buy me dinner or a drink. There are few things more important to our military personnel than a simple, "Thank You."

I understood that dying for our country would be an honor; but letting the enemy die for his country was our duty. My military service took me to Okinawa and mainland Japan, South Korea and the Philippines. For those who believe that our country is not worth standing up for; get a passport and travel the world. I saw no place that I would be willing to call home more than the United States of America. So many take our rights and freedoms for granted and assume that they are the same everywhere in the world. I assure you they are not, and if we continue to allow the erosion of our liberties this will not be the America in which we were raised. President Ronald Reagan was my Commander-in-Chief and the only military conflict worth mentioning during my time of service was Grenada; and it was over before it started. I never saw military combat, but I have the utmost respect for all of those who have.

I also noticed something about the population of Marines that mirrors our society; most every Marine that I knew came from a poor or working class family. This country has been protected by Americans that so often before coming into its service had been left out. The country's control somehow keeps ending up in the hands of wealthy liberals who don't seem to give a damn about it! We must change that practice. If we are going to spend taxpayer money then let's spend it on outfitting our troops to the best of our ability. We must take outstanding care of our veterans and their families.

The Marine Corps experience taught me not only how to be led, but how to lead others. Love of my country, respect for the flag and the knowledge that I was part of something larger than myself was solidified during my service. When I see someone put their political office, wealth or anything else above the safety and security of our nation that pisses me off.

Freedom isn't free and if you ever start to forget that; go and take a walk through one of our National cemeteries. There is no need to do anything but, RESPECT IT! There is no need to say anything more than THANK YOU!

Chapter 3

THE TRUTH DISTORTED

"Everything you can imagine is real" (Picasso n.d.) – Pablo Picasso

In 1905, thirty-two prominent, outspoken African Americans met to discuss the challenges facing people of color and possible strategies and solutions. (The Niagra Movement 2014) Among the issues they were concerned about was the disenfranchisement of blacks in the South starting in 1890 and in 1908. Southern state's legislatures ratified new constitutions creating barriers to voter registration and more complex election rules. (The Niagara Movement 2014) Voter registration and turnout dropped markedly in the South as a result. Men who had been voting for 30 years were told they did not "qualify" to register.

The group struggled for a time with limited resources and internal conflict and disbanded. Because hotels in the United States were segregated, the men convened under the leadership of Harvard scholar W. E. B. Du Bois at a hotel (Fort Erie Hotel) on the Canadian side of Niagara Falls in Fort

Erie, Ontario. As a result, the group came to be known as the Niagara Movement. (The Niagra Movement 2014) A year later, three whites joined the group: journalist William E. Walling, social worker Mary White Ovington, and social worker Henry Moskowitz, then Associate Leader of the New York Society for Ethical Culture in 1910. Many members of the Niagara Movement went on to join the NAACP. Although both organizations shared membership and overlapped in their existence, the Niagara Movement was a separate organization and is historically thought of as having a more radical platform than the NAACP. The Niagara Movement was formed exclusively by African Americans, while the meeting which birthed the idea of the NAACP was comprised of three white people. (The Niagra Movement 2014)

Mary White Ovington, journalist William English Walling and Henry Moskowitz met in New York City in January 1909 and the NAACP was born. (The Niagra Movement 2014)

Now let me get this straight! The National Association for the Advancement of Colored People was founded primarily by three white people. How many blacks have any idea of this fact? How many white and black democrats don't want this fact to be known? It looks like Mama's advice of what's right is right bears true. There is more than enough blame to go around when it comes to some of the racial ills suffered in this country. Most African slaves were sold along the Ivory Coast to white and **black slave traders** by other black Africans. If we are going to have a conversation about race we can't leave anyone out who was involved. Today many white Americans suffer from "white guilt" about the sins of their ancestors, and many of those folks supported Barack Obama in his presidential bids.

While we are looking at facts that are not well known about the history of racism in the United States, I feel compelled to share some facts which are not well publicized, but are readily available to anyone seeking the truth.

After signing the historic Civil Rights Act of 1964, Lyndon Johnson was quoted as saying the following to two sitting governors, aboard Air Force One: **"I'll have those niggers voting Democratic for the next 200 years."** (Huffington Post 2011)

Likewise, we have another lesser known quote from Johnson: **"These Negroes, they're getting pretty uppity these days and that's a problem for us since they've got something now they never had before, the political pull to back up their uppityness. Now we've got to do something about this, we've got to give them a little something, just enough to quiet them down, not enough to make a difference. For if we don't move at all, then their allies will line up against us and there'll be no way of stopping them, we'll lose the filibuster and there'll be no way of putting a brake on all sorts of wild legislation. It'll be Reconstruction all over again."** (Caro 2003)

Far from the image that Democrats would like to portray, Lyndon Baines Johnson didn't have the best interests of African Americans in mind. In fact, the Democrat Party was the home of some of the most bitter and hateful racists, who have totally deceived America when it comes to the history of racial justice.

"Mr. President, the crime of lynching . . . is not of sufficient importance to justify this legislation." (Pepper (D., Fla.), 1938 2009)

Going back a little further in time, the Democrats documented their racism in the Democrat Party Platform: "Instead

of restoring the Union, it [the Republican Party] has, so far as in its power, dissolved it, and subjected ten states, in time of profound peace, to military despotism and Negro supremacy."
–Platform of the Democratic Party, 1868 (Jackson 2009)

One of the longest serving Democrats proudly said this in 1946: ""I am a former Kleagle [recruiter] of the Ku Klux Klan in Raleigh County . . . The Klan is needed today as never before and I am anxious to see its rebirth here in West Virginia. It is necessary that the order be promoted immediately and in every state in the union." (Huffington Post 2011)

That great crusader for civil rights, Bobby Kennedy said this in 1961: "I did not lie awake at night worrying about the problems of Negroes." (Bartlett 2007)

Let us not forget that later Kennedy authorized wiretapping the phones and bugging the hotel rooms of Dr. Martin Luther King, Jr. (Bartlett 2007)

There is voluminous evidence that the Democrat Party sought to discriminate against Blacks, yet somehow they have been able to deny those charges and convinced multitudes that they were the Party of racial equality.

We must be clear with the facts of our history. President Abraham Lincoln signed the Emancipation Proclamation on January 1, 1863 during the Civil War using his war powers privilege (The Niagra Movement 2014). The impact of that event didn't reach Texas until June 19, 1865 when the news arrived in Galveston. (www.juneteenth.com n.d.) To this day Juneteenth is still celebrated in parts of the south as Black Independence Day. The Emancipation Proclamation was not a law passed by congress; but was an executive order instituted by **Abraham Lincoln, who was our first Republican president.**

That is one executive order with which I am very pleased. I have spoken to some blacks who believe that President Lincoln was a Democrat because he freed the slaves. President Lincoln's decision to free the slaves tore this country apart and caused father to fight against their sons and brothers to fight against their brothers. President Lincoln saw slavery as a poison that would kill this nation. Can you think of any other war that had more personal motives in play for some than the Civil War?

Before it's all said and done, Barack Obama may very well have set the wheels in motion to tear this country apart. Obama has made more people than ever before believe that the government is in the business of taking care of them. What is going to happen when all the government giveaways are gone? Do you think those folks who suddenly have no government freebies coming to them are going to be happy?

The ugly truth is there is just as much racism amongst black Americans as there is amongst white Americans. My prayer is that one day soon we can just be Americans. As a law enforcement officer for most of my adult life I have come to realize that there are "turds" (that's a law enforcement term) of every creed and color. We would all be smart to be honest with one another and most importantly treat one another with respect. Many years ago I gave this idea a name; "The Bomb Theory". If you placed a bomb in the middle of a room filled with people of all ethnicities and it detonated, who would be killed? The simple truth is that the bomb would not discriminate and as people neither should we.

In the summer of 2001, I joined the Harris County Sheriff's Office in Houston, Texas. I had an occasion to work an overtime shift in the jail with another black deputy in a two-deputy housing maximum security tank. We had eight hours to get to know one another because the inmates were only allowed to be out in the day area, one at a time. We discussed our backgrounds and after detailing my military, business and law enforcement experience he suggested that I join an organization at the Sheriff's Office known as the Afro-American League (AAL). I'd heard a few things about the organization, but asked him to tell me more. He went on to explain to me that the AAL was all about making sure that black deputies were not railroaded by the current administration. I had heard a few stories about the treatment of blacks by the Sheriff at that time, but had not witnessed any personally. I asked him what else the AAL did and he told me that they were a union and looked out for the best interest of the black members.

Well this is where I probably lost the opportunity to make a new friend. I asked this deputy what would happen if the white deputies got together and formed a white deputy's organization? He immediately snapped, "Oh we got that already around here, it's the Klan." I asked him if he had ever worked on the streets as a police office and he said that he had not. I asked him if he were in a fight and had to call for other deputies; would he care what race the deputies were that came to help him. He immediately told me that it wouldn't matter to him. I told him that my entire law enforcement career had been on the streets and the race of an officer coming to save your life was completely irrelevant. I gave him the advice my mother had given me long ago; "what's right is right, what's wrong is wrong, no matter who's doing it." This deputy hasn't had much to say to me over the years, but what's right is right. Racism is wrong and if we all realize that and fight together it would be closer to ending.

In 2009 a member of the Harris County Sheriff's Office founded the Caucasian Law Enforcement Association (CLEA). According to the founder of the group he only created the organization to have a seat at the table with the administration. There is undoubtedly a need in law enforcement to have an organization that looks out for the best interest of law enforcement officers. There are few things more dangerous in government or law enforcement than an unchecked administration. I just don't believe it needs to be a group with the need to be linked to or identified by race.

Chapter 4

MEETING A PAYROLL

"If you don't know where you are going, any road will get you there." (Carroll 2008) – Lewis Carroll

There is much wisdom in the old adage give a man a fish and he will eat for the day; but teaching a man to fish will allow him to eat for a lifetime. As of the writing of this book approximately forty seven percent of Americans pay no income tax at all. Presidential candidate Mitt Romney said this during the 2012 presidential campaign and was attacked, but it's true. Why does the truth make some people so angry? This violates the basic principles of fairness, that so many people pay no taxes. If this disparity continues; where will it stop? Will 25% pay all the taxes with 75% paying none? Do the liberals ever stop to think what will happen when there is nothing else "free" to give?

In 1993 I made a decision while living in San Diego, California to leave law enforcement to test the private sector. I was a Police Sergeant for the City of National City, California, making a high five figure salary with great benefits. I wanted more and knew that if I worked hard I could achieve anything. I had an opportunity to get into the mortgage industry and subsequently the real estate business. I obtained my California Real Estate Broker's License in 1996. The mortgage industry came quite naturally to me.

In three years I had learned enough about both industries; mortgage and real estate and decided to merge the two. I founded the Pittman Company, Real Estate & Mortgage Services. I found what many business owners have found and that is the amount of government red tape makes business much tougher to do. Between licensing fees, regulatory fees & requirements, federal, state and local taxes, it is a daily challenge for businesses to do business. What company is anxious to hire when profits are constantly consumed by government? Making a payroll is something most politicians don't understand. I recognized before my first day in business that meeting my professional responsibilities to my employees and associates had to be a first line priority. I never missed a payroll and always kept my word.

I don't understand electing someone to a legislative position to make rules over business when that individual has no or poor business experience. This is how we wound up with Barack Obama as President of the United States. Obama was a community activist who was elected to the U.S. Senate from Illinois and had no business experience what so ever. Then with two years as a Senator he was elected to the presidency. Experience does not always ensure success, but it is a very important asset to have in your bag.

As a broker I owed a fiduciary responsibility to my clients and placed their interest above my own. Can you imagine if government operated in this fashion and placed our interests above theirs? We can have just that if we demand it. We must hold elected officials responsible and kick their butts out of office whenever they don't live up to their promises. We have come to expect the worse from the "ruling class" and it is time for that to change. We need to raise our expectations and hold these men and women to the same standards that "We the people" are held. I propose that Congress and the Senate lose all benefits each year they do not pass a balanced budget. Do you think that might motivate them? I propose that no member of Congress or the Senate may derive any income from any source other than their government paycheck. Finally, all members of Congress and the Senate need to be subjected to the laws they pass, just as the citizens they represent! Do you think Congress has an entitlement mentality?

As a high school junior in 1979 I first saw the real life poisonous effects of the entitlement mentality. I was sitting in the gymnasium one afternoon waiting on a pep rally to begin. There were two young black female students sitting in the bleachers just above me. I heard one of them say, "Well I'm going to have three!" I wasn't sure of what she was talking about; but as she continued speaking it became very clear. She explained that her sister had two children and received $374.00 per child or ($758 monthly) and she went on to explain her plan that if she had three children she could "make" $1122.00 monthly.

I could not believe what I had just heard; her plan for her financial future was to have three children for the for the sole purpose of making money, at whose expense? You guessed it, the taxpayer's! As you can see this was a learned behavior, this young girl was apparently planning to do what she had seen done in her home. That told me that a good positive environment was very important when planning life decisions.

Let me say that there is nothing wrong with accepting help when you need it. I believe that we have a moral obligation to help those who **cannot** help themselves, the elderly, the mentally challenged and the very young. My Holy Bible, in **Deuteronomy 15:11** states: "**There will always be poor people in the land. Therefore I command you to be open-handed toward your brothers and toward the <u>poor</u> and <u>needy</u> in your land.**" But, even the Holy Bible holds the lazy accountable in **2 Thessalonians 3:10** by stating: "**If a man will not work, he shall not eat.**" Manipulating the social system for financial gain, in my opinion, should be illegal and in some cases it is, but politicians are using the promise of entitlements to fuel their vote totals. There is virtually nothing in place to hold people accountable for abusing the system. The liberal Democrat believes that we should give everything to everyone, but I have yet to hear a liberal explain what we do when there is nothing left to give away. Margaret Thatcher put it this way: "The problem with socialism is that eventually you run out of other people's money [to spend]." (Attributed to Thatcher 2013)

The liberal politicians maintain the poor's vote by giving them shelter, food, medical, even free cell phones with service (e.g. Obamaphones)! The poor are given everything except the incentive to better their station in life. This is unfair to the poor, but ultimately more unfair to the taxpayers who are stuck footing the bill for the never ending stream of entitlements. As previously stated 47% of Americans are paying no income taxes. (Urban Institute, Brookings Institution, n.d.) I'm no constitutional lawyer, but one could argue that it seems to violate the Equal Protection Clause of the 14th Amendment. The rest of us are left to pay for those who don't want to work, but want everything provided for them, as the girl in the gymnasium who was going to improve upon her sisters' economic plan by having three children for the social relief provided.

If we do not stop this it will destroy us. Just as anything else it will take time to wean those who have become accustomed to this lifestyle off of it. Is there a better time than right now to start? We can continue to concern ourselves with being "politically correct" or we can say, no more, get your lazy butts to work! **Lazy isn't a color it's an attitude!**

Chapter 5

ENFORCING THE LAW AND PROTECTING OUR COUNTRY

―∞―

"Life's tough. It's tougher when you're stupid." – (J. a. Wayne, Sands of Iwo Jima 1949) John Wayne

P otentially one of the most dangerous failures in our country today is the failure to protect our borders. The illegal alien population in the United States in 2011 was estimated to be 11 million. Somehow that reported number never seems to get any larger. In my opinion we have 3 to 5 million illegals in Texas alone. That number, I believe, is grossly understated and is most likely between 20 and 30 million. I ran for Sheriff in Harris County (Houston) Texas in 2012 and lost in the Republican run off. I was endorsed by Sheriff Joe Arpaio of Maricopa County, Arizona. Sheriff Joe Arpaio is the face of enforcement against illegal aliens and has come under constant fire from the liberal left; mainly the Eric Holder-led Justice Department under the Obama Administration. As of the writing of this book, the U.S. Justice Department has recently dropped the case against Arpaio. I wonder why? If they had a case against Joe Arpaio they would have built a new prison to put him in. Laws are intended to be mandates, not options. If we have bad laws then we should all be screaming and working to eliminate them. But if the laws are constitutional they should be enforced without prejudice.

Figure 9 Sheriff Joe and Carl in Phoenix

Figure 10 Tent City Jail – Maricopa County, AZ

I do not believe that Barack Obama wants to be President of the United States. I believe Barack Hussein Obama wants to be "King" of the United States. It will not surprise me if he makes an attempt to somehow circumvent the 22nd Amendment to the U. S. Constitution to seek additional terms as president. Obama believes if he can coddle illegals then he can continue to build his voter base amongst Latinos. Only time will tell if this works. This same mentality exists among some Republicans who are afraid that taking action will anger Latinos and they will somehow magically become Democrats. Many Latinos are as upset over the illegal alien problems as non-Latinos. Latinos as well as others would be upset and rightfully so if Latinos were being prosecuted by the police solely on their appearance. We live in a country of laws and excusing law breakers is a road we shouldn't travel.

Sheriff Arpaio had been accused of racial profiling and just about everything else under the sun in never ending, ongoing federal investigations. Why is this being done to a man who is simply upholding his oath as the elected Sheriff of his county? Barack Obama should be prosecuted for refusing to live up to his oath of office because he is placing politics above the safety and security of this nation, and that should be a crime. By the way the good citizens of Maricopa County, Arizona had the good sense to re-elect Joe Arpaio to his sixth–four year term as Maricopa County Sheriff in November of 2012.

Barack Obama has refused to uphold his oath of office and has circumvented the legislative process by ruling by "Executive Order" and he should be brought up on articles of impeachment. Obama's illegal act of removing the threat of deportation and allowing hundreds of thousands of illegals to stay in the United States and work further weakens the economy and the rule of law in this country. We have millions of citizens out of work and the president is allowing illegals to stay and compete against American citizens for the available jobs. Is this the kind of "lead by the seat of your pants" representation you want? Obama is convinced that whatever it takes to stay popular is the goal of the day.

Why has Barack Obama continually been given a pass? Why has the liberal media refused to report on real issues involving him? Why is it that the Republican led Congress effectively has done nothing in response to the "Fast and Furious" and Benghazi debacles which have led to the death of a federal officer and embassy staff? Why have all of the valid questions regarding his birth certificate been virtually ignored by the media, who otherwise reports on everything? Can you imagine what would have happened if George W. Bush had done half of the stuff Obama has done?

During the 2012 election I saw a Facebook fundraising advertisement, "African Americans for Obama." There would have been outrage if "Whites for W" had started up during Bush's re-election campaign. Remember Mama's advice: **What's right is right, what's wrong is wrong, no matter who does it!**

Now I'm sure I will be accused of selling out for "the man". The truth is I hate injustice, no matter who is responsible for it. I was critical of George W. Bush when his performance did not meet muster. I'm not too pleased that the Weapons of Mass Destruction were not found and the liberal media made sure we all knew about it. But the difference for me is that I don't believe that George W. Bush lied and that is a huge difference with what I see going on today. Do you think that Obama and Attorney General Holder have been honest about "Fast and Furious" and Benghazi? Don't the families of these American heroes deserve to know the truth about what happened to their loved ones? Again, why does Obama keep getting a pass?

The conservative fight against illegal aliens is not just against the liberal left, it is also against factions within the Republican Party who have continually placed their financial bottom lines above the safety and security of this country. These individuals identify themselves as pro-life, pro-family, less government conservatives; but will fight tooth and nail to protect the "rights" of illegal aliens to "illegally" occupy this country and you know why? MONEY!!!!!!!!

The availability of cheap labor significantly adds to the bottom lines of these individuals and their companies. We are talking about very wealthy people like Texas based homebuilder and one of the country's largest Republican donors, Bob Perry of Perry Homes (now deceased). Businesses exist for the purpose of making money not friends. However, how can profit be placed above our security? Do the American servicemen and servicewomen risk anything less in protecting and defending our nation?

As mentioned earlier, there are those who have spent a great deal of time, money and influence fighting to defeat good legislation such as the Sanctuary Cities Legislation which was before the Texas Legislature in the spring of 2011. I'm not for sale, that was resolved in 1863 and what I believe in is not, nor will ever be for sale. The problem for some is that my belief system doesn't fit their idea that everything is up for sale.

Enforcing the Law and Protecting Our Country

Now in every other situation of which I am aware, many of these supporters of illegal immigration tell the world that they are Christian, pro-life pro-family conservatives, but you can see that this problem of illegal immigration will not soon be solved until we do something very important. FOLLOW THE LAW! If it's bad law or unconstitutional law let's get rid of it. But if it is not, then let's follow the law. When I was a kid I heard about a promise made long ago, that the Mexicans would take back this land without firing a shot. Looks like their strategy may be working, but there have been a few shots fired. Just ask the family of murdered Houston Police Officer Rodney Johnson who was killed by an armed previously deported illegal alien.

The problem with our failure to secure our border is a catastrophe waiting to happen. There are illegals from around the globe entering the four southern Border States, California, Arizona, New Mexico and Texas. The fact that known radical Islamist are training in and around Mexico City should be enough of a reason on its merits to secure the border, but it's not! The fact that Mexican drug cartels are possibly working with terrorist organizations doesn't seem to merit securing the border. The government of the United States should classify the South American and Mexican Cartels as a terrorist threat and deal with them in the same manner as they dealt with Osama Bin Laden and Al Qaeda. We should seek them out and kill them!

The fact that the events of September 11, 2001 have not convinced the leaders of this nation to secure our borders is completely unfathomable. Nearly 3,000 victims died as a result of the 9/11 attacks. This was a mutual failure for both Democrats and Republicans alike. Death is the great equalizer;

it does not consider conservative nor liberal, black nor white, Christian or Atheist.

This country continues to entertain all sorts of outrageous "un-American ideas. Can you believe that "Sharia Law" is slowly creeping into our society? **News Flash!** I don't have a problem with Muslims practicing their beliefs, AS LONG AS THEY ARE DONE IN ACCORDANCE WITH AMERICAN LAW. If Muslims want to do something other than that then they should return to a country where they can practice the way they want. Sharia Law has no respect for women and considers them as nothing more than property. Women can be abused, tortured and even killed without consideration. Sharia Law does not consider a non-Muslim as an equal to a Muslim. This does not reflect American values and no one who calls themselves an American would ever find this acceptable. <u>THIS WAS THE BELIEF OF THOSE WHO CARRIED OUT THE SEPTEMBER 11, 2001 ATTACKS!</u>

One of my real fears is a radiological weapon, a "dirty bomb" being deployed against us. The truth of the matter is that most U. S. cities are not prepared to deal with this threat in a manner that will protect the lives of their citizens. The ingredients to produce these devices are unbelievably easy to acquire for those who would use them. How simple would it be for a terrorist group to deploy multiple dirty bombs in Washington, Houston, Dallas, Los Angeles, New York and Atlanta? The general opinion of these devices is that they are not deployed for their ability to kill large numbers of people, but rather to render the area exposed as uninhabitable and create mass fear and disruption. Now consider Washington, Houston, Dallas, Los Angeles, New York and Atlanta uninhabitable. The result would be devastating to the entire country. Now what price tag would be put on this scale of devastation? Let's see, priceless? We must demand that those elected to serve us take this seriously and do something about it.

As a California Peace Officer in the late 1980's and early 90's illegal aliens were such a part of the San Diego landscape that they were allowed to walk right down the middle barrier of Interstate 5 from San Ysidro to downtown San Diego. Local, State and Federal law enforcement officers were prohibited from interfering with them for fear of the aliens fleeing into traffic and being struck. That even led to the creation of the, "Illegal Alien Crossing Signs" depicted below.

Figure 11 Illegal Alien Crossing Sign Warning in California (1980's)

There are those who continue to argue that Illegal "**Immigrants**" are hard-working, Christian, pro-family and they should be allowed to stay. First and foremost they are ILLEGAL! Their very presence is a violation of the law and a slap in the face of every law abiding American and every person who came to this country and did it the right way! Can you imagine using the argument that we shouldn't lock up bank robbers, because they are just trying to take care of their families? Why don't we post a bank robber parking sign in front of our banks—Sounds pretty stupid right???????

I do not fault illegals for wanting to get here. I fault government leadership for not addressing their illegal arrival and illegal occupancy!

Chapter 6

BLACK LEADERS OR SELF-APPOINTED BLACK LEADERS

"A leader is one who knows the way, goes the way, and shows the way." (Maxwell 2010)– John C. Maxwell

Dr. Martin Luther King was a true leader. He called for peace and justice and knew that the best route to equality was by opportunity for all Americans. Dr. King was a **Republican** as were many American Blacks in that era. Why you ask? The Republican Party was founded in 1854 as the anti-slavery party a decade before our first Republican President Abraham Lincoln signed the Emancipation Proclamation. The Republican Party has long fought for freedom and civil rights for blacks. Today so many black Americans are living in a distorted reality. Many blacks believe that the Democratic Party is the Party of the people when the truth is there have been few influences in the history of this country as destructive to blacks as the ideology of the Democratic Party. The Democratic Party has done very little if anything to actually help get blacks from under government dependence. When President Obama was identified as the "Food Stamp King" Republicans were called racist, but the facts don't lie. The number of individuals on food stamps has absolutely exploded under Obama and many of those people getting food stamps are simply manipulating the system. You can even get a free cell phone under the giveaway policies of Obama. Where will it stop?

In complete contradiction to what most blacks believe, the Democratic Party has been the party of the "S's".

SLAVERY
SECESSION
SEGREGATION

And now a fourth, SOCIALISM, under the direction of Barack Obama! Poor people, particularly blacks in America have been voting Democrat for decades based upon the belief that the Democratic Party is going to improve their lives. But most of those blacks are no better off than the generations that preceded them.

It was the Democrats that fought the Civil War to keep blacks in slavery and passed the discriminatory Black Codes and the unfair Jim Crow Laws. (Dr. David Pilgrim 2012). It was the Democrats who promoted and protected the Ku Klux Klan, to lynch and terrorize blacks during and after the end of slavery. (KKK Terrorist Arm of the Democratic Party 2009) The KKK still exists today, closer to home than you might suspect. Democrats fought against the passage of every civil rights law starting with the civil rights laws of the 1860's, and continuing into the 1950's and 1960's.

However, it was Republican President Dwight D. Eisenhower who pushed to pass the Civil Rights Act of 1957 and sent federal troops to Arkansas to desegregate schools. (Eisenhower and the Little Rock Crisis n.d.) The facts matter!

Reverend Al "The Race Baiter" Sharpton can find racism everywhere. If a tragedy befalls a black anywhere in the country to where the media is willing to travel, he'll be there. Leaders lead before, during and after something happens, they don't need an incident to lead.

Take a look at Colonel Allen B. West, former U. S. Representative from the 22nd District in Florida. Congressman West tells it like it is and isn't so concerned about being politically correct. He has served his country as a U.S. Army Officer in combat and the most important thing of all; he is committed to protecting and defending the U. S. Constitution. When did protecting and defending our Constitution become a bad thing? The opposition went to great lengths to defeat him in his 2012 re-election bid.

Now in stark contrast: is Reverend Al Sharpton a black leader? When was the election? I must have missed it! I don't remember the election of Al Sharpton to lead me anywhere! We just might get a true glimpse of Al Sharpton who starred in an undercover DEA drug deal video some years ago trying to set up a cocaine delivery, but never mind; he felt "threatened". If Al Sharpton was "threatened" in that video tape then he has truly missed his calling, and he should be in Hollywood. Well, he's close, as he became the host of his own daily political talk show "PoliticsNation" on MSNBC in 2011.

The National Action Network, based in New York, was founded by Reverend Al Sharpton in 1991. (Sharpton 2011) That organization brings in large sums of money annually to supposedly further its agenda of addressing the social and economic inequalities suffered by blacks in the United States. That's all well and good, but in my opinion the reverend doesn't seem to do much more than to seek out incidents around the country that are high in media coverage where the race card can be easily played. He then uses some of these tragedies to encourage donations to the NAN (National Action Network). Was MSNBC scraping the bottom of the journalistic barrel to highlight Sharpton as the host of his own show, "PoliticsNation?" Sharpton wouldn't criticize President Obama regardless of what was happening. This is exactly why as Republicans, when a member of our party "steps in it" let's call it for what it is. We do nothing but lose credibility when we try and look away.

On the night of February 26, 2012 in Sanford, Florida a 17 year old black youth, Trayvon Martin, was shot to death by George Zimmerman. (CNN Political Unit 2013) This was a tragedy if for nothing more than the loss of life for a 17 year old young man. Zimmerman was a 28 year old multi-racial man who while out running some errands saw Martin walking through the gated community. Zimmerman was the "Neighborhood Watch Coordinator" in that gated community and became involved in a confrontation with Martin that resulted in Martin being shot and killed. I was not present during this confrontation and guess what, neither was Al Sharpton. As a veteran peace officer I know the importance of not jumping to conclusions. It is a tragic thing for any child to be killed and it is unfortunate that the young man's death became an opportunity for Sharpton and others to perpetuate their special style, or lack of "black leadership."

The Martin incident called for a thorough and fair investigation to find the facts, not threats of riots and violence. What was the age old chant used, "No Justice, No Peace?" How can you have justice without an investigation to determine what has occurred? How can you have an investigation when those charged with carrying out the investigations are being threatened with keeping their jobs? **Is this not in part the same mob mentality that plagued the Old Jim Crow South that "justified" the hanging of countless blacks?** What's right is right and what's wrong is wrong, no matter who does it!

Sheila Jackson-Lee, Texas Congresswoman for the 18th Congressional District is known for her bright attire (to ensure that she can be seen easily on television) during State of the Union Addresses. The running joke is not to get caught between her and a camera or you are going to get hurt. In the summer of 2005 while assigned as an Internal Affairs Division (IAD) Investigator for the Harris County Sheriff's Office I was assigned to investigate a tragic shooting involving a Sheriff's Deputy and an off-duty Reserve Deputy Constable. The Deputy Constable was shot and killed after an unfortunate series of events while working an extra job as a security guard in an apartment complex in northeast Harris County Texas.

I arrived on the scene at approximately 2:45 that morning and found most of the Houston television news affiliates on the scene. So often when a minority is shot by law enforcement there is a rush to claim police misconduct. This is why the police must be well trained, equipped, and professional. Proper training is the least expensive insurance in the police business.

The scene investigation was subsequently completed and while all officer involved shootings are investigated by homicide units for criminal reasons, they are also administratively investigated by the Internal Affairs Division (IAD) of the employing agency of the officer(s) who discharged their weapon(s). Now let's get back to the Congresswoman. For the next several business days following the shooting the Congresswoman called the IAD office trying to get information. Now I'm not psychic, but I had a pretty good idea of exactly what she wanted. No official identification or ethnicity of the Sheriff's Deputy had been released to the public. I knew that it was highly improbable that the Congresswoman was a witness to the shooting so returning or taking her call was not a major priority in the completion of my official duties.

I finally spoke with her about a week after the shooting. The Congresswoman immediately began to ask for information that would not have been proper to release. I then decided to test my theory by telling Congresswoman Jackson-Lee that the Sheriff's Deputy who had shot the Deputy Constable was also black. Well bluntly put, you could have heard a fly fart on the phone; there was complete silence for a moment and as you can imagine that is no small feat, silencing the Congresswoman. But it confirmed my theory, she was not concerned with the incident for any other reason but to see if there was a racial spin she could put on it. That phone call was terminated with no further questions or calls. The case was completed and ultimately presented to a grand jury which returned a "no-bill" clearing the deputy of any criminal wrongdoing.

Chapter 7

ENTITLEMENTS

"If we can but prevent the government from wasting the labors of the people, under the pretense of taking care of them, they must become happy" (Jefferson, Home › Jefferson › Quotations › Famous Quotations n.d.) – Thomas Jefferson

Politics so often comes down to economics, not ideology. Have you ever heard the phrase, "Politics makes for strange bed fellows?" The Democratic Party has gotten a large segment of the population "hooked" on entitlements. This is the political version of the modern day drug dealer. In the mid 1980's when crack cocaine hit the scene the street drug dealers grew their client base by giving the drugs to new customers. Crack cocaine was so incredibly addictive, that the new customers became hooked almost immediately and would then do anything for the drug. The new drug addicts would do anything to get the "currency" to pay the dealer for the drug that started out as being free; murder, prostitution, theft; mothers would even sell their children to feed their habit!

Now let us compare this marketing strategy to what the Democratic Party has done. Entitlements have been given and as the "customers" become addicted to the entitlements, they will do anything to continue getting them. The currency required to continue getting entitlements isn't money per se, it's the VOTE!

<u>Community Activists</u>

Every major city in the U.S. has those self-described Community Activists. Yes we even have a few in Houston, Texas; I will not list the names of these individuals because they do not deserve any attention. I bring this up only to say these two things: if you are a community activist you should show up to assist victims, regardless of the race of any alleged victim. A black activist only showing up when the victim is black hurts the credibility of the activist; a true activist should show up regardless of the race of any victim.

In the aftermath of a 2008 New Year's Eve police shooting of a young black man in Bellaire, Texas a local activist as reported by KHOU TV Channel 11 stated, **"If you shoot one more black in Bellaire, your city will go up in flames"**. Now this statement is probably protected by the 1st Amendment and I do fully support the Constitution, but this is a dangerous statement that could have sparked riots. I was a police Sergeant in Southern California during the Rodney King riots and trust me you don't want that coming to your city.

I have nothing but the utmost respect for anyone who has enough concern for their community to step up and get involved, but do it because it's the right thing to do, not to showboat or intentionally cause more problems. Does the good book say in

Matthew 5:16 – " Let your light so shine before men, that they may see your good works, and glorify YOU?" I think not!

It says, "Let your light so shine before men, that they may see your good works, and glorify your **Father which is in heaven.**"

A prime example of why community activists need to act responsibly when it comes to police investigations is the 2010 Chad Holley case in Houston, Texas. Chad Holley had committed a burglary and was being pursued by the Houston Police Department. (The Associated Press 2013) Holley was eventually cornered just outside the fence of a storage business that captured the event on surveillance video. Holley attempted to leap over the front of a patrol unit and fell to the ground. Holley laid flat on his stomach and placed his hands out to his side. Several HPD officers simultaneously made it to his location and well, let's say they didn't sing him happy birthday. Holley was subsequently taken into custody with several bumps and bruises. Holley was found guilty of burglary and was placed on probation, until he turned eighteen. Holley's conduct was quickly written off as a youthful mistake.

Four of the Houston Police Officers involved in the arrest were subsequently fired and criminally charged with assaulting Holley. I am not condoning police misconduct and there is no place in law enforcement for brutality. A professional law enforcement officer must always obey the law and never let their personal feelings enter into their professional decisions. It's not always easy, but it is necessary.

I have an interesting hypothesis though; had young Mr. Holley not been out committing a burglary his story wouldn't even be in this book. I am absolutely sure those police officers would not have gone to his house and assaulted him while he was doing his homework. Holley's mother didn't seem too interested in the fact that her son was a burglar, but was quick to locate an attorney to pursue a big tax free civil suit. Mr. Holley should have grown up in my house and gotten a "taste" or two. The simple truth is that Chad Holley was a burglar, who needed to get whipped; it just should have happened at home.

That same local "community activist" from the Bellaire Police shooting incident acquired the Holly video surveillance after a judge had barred its release by the prosecution and released it to the local broadcast media. The local minority community was in an uproar and rightfully so. From the content of the video; it didn't look good. Houston's Police Chief and Mayor were all over the media criticizing the officers and bowed to public pressure. The four officers were fired without a trial or any admission of guilt. This was a professional death sentence to these four officers. I am not justifying their actions, but isn't this the United States of America? What happened to due process? The release of that video could only serve a couple of purposes; taint the potential jury pool and/or spark civil unrest. There was a reason the judge barred the release of the video, and since it was released, the consequences had to be dealt with. In my opinion there was every reason to have granted a change of venue for the trial. Now, had a change of venue been granted due to the release of the video that same activist would have been outraged. Justice was not wanted; only the desired verdict.

Andrew Blomberg was the first officer tried and subsequently acquitted. I was not present for trial and was not privileged to see the evidence presented. Black community leaders were up in arms and called the verdict unjust and, here we go, "racist". Would this have been the same reaction had Blomberg been found guilty, because the video would have surely had an effect on the local jury pool? Why was the release of the video not criticized by these same community leaders? Many will argue that past transgressions suffered by blacks should justify these things; but I disagree. Remember "what's right is right and what's wrong is wrong". I am so grateful that my mother instilled that in me!

As a footnote, Chad Holley was arrested again for burglary in 2012 and guess who escorted him out of jail? That same community activist who would later be the target of allegations of "ripping" off blacks that he was supposedly helping. What message does this send? Well I guess accountability is a racial thing.

Chapter 8

POLICE LEGITIMACY AND ACCOUNTABILITY

"The superior man acts before he speaks, and afterwards speaks according to his actions. (Confucius n.d.)"
– Confucius

My career in law enforcement began in August of 1985 after my honorable discharge from the United States Marine Corps. I entered the 103rd Regional San Diego Police Academy in the summer of 1985 and, as many young police cadets, I was convinced that I could change the world. The police academy was an easy transition coming from the Marine Corps, but I was eager to learn everything necessary to become the best police officer possible.

Criminal Law was incredibly interesting to me; it along with constitutional law made perfect sense to me. The fact that the police have to work within boundaries and the criminal element did not was a great challenge. The police had to be the good guys because society depends on the police to keep the peace and to maintain a sense of order. The very fact of having the full force and effect of the law behind me as a police officer gave me a great sense of pride; but it also created a great deal of responsibility.

Police Legitimacy and Accountability

In order for the public to support police action the police must constantly prove their actions are lawful and be ready to stand accountable for their decisions, both good and bad. The "letter of the law" versus the "spirit of the law" is a constant test that each police officer must use in completing their duties. For years the posted speed limit on most U. S. roadways was 55 mph. The "letter of the law" enforcement would call for an officer to issue speeding citations for drivers traveling 56 mph or faster. Now most fair minded people would say that is too tight and would hope that officers would allow some sort of allowance for minor speed differences.

It was always my practice to account for the totality of the situation before issuing a ticket. It was my belief that the primary goal of police action was to keep the public safe, not be a source of revenue for the government. When police enforcement makes sense to the public, the public will accept the action. The trust given to police officers is of the highest order and all steps must be taken to maintain it!

In 1986 in San Diego County, California one of the most disturbing cases of police misconduct imaginable occurred. On the night of December 27, 1986, 20 year old college student Cara Knott was driving home from an evening at her boyfriend's home in Escondido, California, just north of San Diego. She was driving south on Interstate 15 towards her home in El Cajon, California (McMurran 1988). When she did not show up her parents became worried and alerted the authorities.

A search ensued and her vehicle was located at the Mercy Road off ramp of southbound I-15. Her body was subsequently located in the rocky ravine below. California Highway Patrol Officer Craig Peyer was identified as a suspect after he was reported to have conducted traffic stops on other young women and directed them to that same location. In 1988 Craig Peyer was convicted of murder and sentenced to 25 years to life in prison. (Petrillo 2004) As of the writing of this book Peyer was recently denied parole and is not eligible for another hearing until 2027.

As a result of that case, female motorists were afraid to stop for law enforcement and were given free passes to continue to well-lit areas before stopping. Can you imagine how the "crooks" took advantage of this? We had more "slow failure to yields" than you could imagine while evidence was tossed from vehicles and crooks planned their encounters with the police. This was a sad day for law enforcement.

The most important thing that the police can do is to hold themselves to the same standards to which they hold the public. The public hates seeing a police car speed past without lights and siren. Why? If the citizen sped past the officer enforcement action would be taken. That is why the police must hold themselves accountable and be held to a higher standard because of the awesome power they hold.

Most Americans who saw the Rodney King video tape beating found it disturbing. I think the general public would have had a much different reaction if the police had taken Rodney King into custody sooner instead of continuing to beat him long after he could have been handcuffed. The fact that the officers did not hold themselves accountable in the completion of their duties caused a black eye for the profession. The $3,800,000.00 dollars paid by the taxpayers of the City of Los Angeles (Rodney King, key L.A. riots figure, dead at 47 2012) to Rodney King could have and should have been avoided.

Law Enforcement Administrators elected and appointed need to constantly remain vigilant in keeping their agency policy updated with recent court decisions and best practices for the profession. Administrators must always remember that their duty to protect and serve the public is just as important as being fair and lawful in their dealings with employees of their respective agencies.

As an Internal Affairs Investigator during my law enforcement career I was responsible for investigating alleged wrongdoings by other police officers. The purpose of an investigation is to collect the facts and let the facts take you wherever they lead. No investigation should be conducted with the intent to prove or disprove an allegation. Just the facts!

The awesome authority granted to law enforcement and prosecutors must come with significant accountability. The intentional misconduct of a law enforcement official or prosecutor during the completion of their official duties should never be tolerated and should be dealt with as a serious criminal matter. This is an important way to hold the profession accountable and maintain legitimacy within the public eye.

I have saved the simplest but most important detail for last………WE ALL MUST FOLLOW THE LAW! The badge is not just a symbol of authority, but it is an acceptance of the public trust to do what is right even if it is not popular.

Chapter 9

POLITICS MIRRORS REAL LIFE – THERE ARE NO PERFECT PEOPLE

"Fall seven times, Get up eight." (Japanese proverbs 2013) – Japanese Proverb

Politics is a microcosm of life. Everything that happens in life happens in politics. The worst of human behavior can be found in the political arena. On December 15, 2000 in Atlanta, Georgia, Derwin Brown, a DeKalb County Police Department Captain, was the Sheriff-elect of DeKalb County, Georgia. Brown was assassinated in the driveway by his defeated rival Sidney Dorsey (Former Sheriff Guilty in Successor's Killing July).

Remember Anthony Weiner the U. S. Representative from New York's 9th District who was forced to resign from Congress after a sexting scandal? Weiner told every story in the book, even had the FBI investigating whether he had been hacked. The truth is Weiner was sexting and didn't want the world to know – can you blame him? My question is why was he allowed to keep his congressional pension after lying to federal investigators?

How about in 2008 when then Governor of New York, Eliot Spitzer, was forced to step down after his ongoing involvement with high priced prostitutes? Now strangely enough Spitzer (also known as "Client 9") had made his rise in politics in New York by promising that "ethics and integrity would be the hallmarks of his administration." There are no perfect people and when you expect perfection from another human being you are only setting yourself up for disappointment.

MUDSLINGING

Do you have any idea how many potentially great leaders are among us, but will never run for political office because of the brutal nature of politics? Does it really matter if someone has been divorced? Does it really matter if a 50 year old candidate skipped a day of school when they were in high school? Attacks on a candidate's family should be off limits; a candidate that doesn't respect that is not prepared to lead. If a candidate cannot keep to the issues related to the office they seek then that candidate should not be worthy of your vote. Remember the attacks that Republican Presidential Candidate Herman Cain came under? I have met Herman Cain on several occasions and have no idea if the rumors of an extra-marital affair were true; but if they were, the concern was surely between him and his wife and Jesus Christ. He wasn't doing it on the governments' dime or the governments' time.

Figure12 Herman and Carl, 2011 Bay Area Republican Women Annual Dinner

The attacks against Republican Presidential nominee Mitt Romney were brutal, even going so far as to attack his Mormon faith. Mitt Romney is a good American, active in his church and a generous and caring man. Now the sad thing about the mudslinging is that this was launched by other Republicans. Some of these same attacks were refocused against Romney in the general election. Do you think the other side isn't just waiting for us to destroy and weaken one-another to help them? We can change this by absolutely turning our backs on any candidate who plays by these rules.

I saw it in my 2012 campaign when my opponents and some of their overzealous supporters attacked my wife and even my children. Do you want a candidate who will claim to support family values, but have such little respect for the family? Ask yourself how you would want to be treated? How often do we end up with primary winners that can't win a general election? Voting for a primary candidate that cannot win is like building a boat that will not float. Both of these things are a complete waste of time.

Chapter 10

THE U.S. CONSTITUTION AND OUR FOUNDING DOCUMENTS

"The tree of liberty must be refreshed from time to time with the blood of patriots and tyrants" (Jefferson, A Little Rebellion Now and Then Is A Good Thing A Letter From Thomas Jefferson To James Madison 1787)
– Thomas Jefferson

The founding fathers were fleeing the tyrannical rule of King George III of England. Patrick Henry is famous for the quote, "Give me liberty or give me death!" He and others risked it all for liberty and freedom from tyranny. Now I will say this early, as perfect as the founding documents are, there was one overwhelming flaw; <u>they did not address and outlaw slavery</u>. The ownership of one human being by another is inherently wrong and the rape of women, separation of families, beatings, and inhumane treatment during and after transport to America was surely against God's law. This is in my opinion the most painful and embarrassing episode in American history. Many blacks believe to this day that the federal government has not properly dealt with the aftermath of slavery. When I was a young boy I remember hearing some of the elders talk about never getting their forty acres and a mule.

One of the most interesting ideas that came out of the last stages of the Civil War during 1865 was "40 Acres and a Mule". This was a short-lived policy of giving land to black former slaves who had become free as a result of the advance of the Union Army into the territory that had previously been under the control of the Confederacy. Union Army Major General William Tecumseh issued Special Order No. 15 on January 16, 1865 that provided for land and some of the newly freed slave landowners to receive mules from the U.S. Army for use in farming.

The Special Order issued by General Tecumseh was never intended to be the official policy of the government. But some black folks even to this day will talk about getting their forty acres and a mule. Well if it ever happens; I want 40 acres on New York's Park Avenue and a Gulfstream G650!

First and foremost, the Constitution is not a living and changing document! <u>It says what it says and it means what it says!</u> We should not disregard it or change it on a whim to suit the needs or desires of certain groups. The only thing that maintains America as that shining light on the hill is the will of her patriots to protect and defend her.

In a recent address to congressional colleagues, Sheila Jackson Lee (D-Texas) illustrated her ignorance of the constitution when she boldly asserted on the floor of the House of Representatives, that the constitution and the American system of governance has lasted about 400 years—insinuating that our guiding legal document was signed around 1614. Her statement is a reflection of the lack of relevance she feels that the constitution holds in her value system. (Chumley 2014)

Our founding documents clearly call for three branches of government; the Executive, Legislative and Judicial. The separation of powers was clearly installed with the intention to never return to a "monarch" style of government. Barack Obama has chosen to overlook the separation of powers. On June 15, 2012 Barack Obama signed the executive order effectively granting amnesty to certain illegal aliens in this country (Preston and Cushman Jr. 2012). This is a direct violation of the law and outside his authority to do, but Congress would need to act in order to stop it. As of this writing Congress has failed to act and the congress is controlled by Republicans and the Senate by the Democrats.

There has been no time more important than now in our country's history to protect and preserve the constitution. I am a member of the National Rifle Association and a staunch supporter of the 2nd Amendment. A well-armed populous is a strong deterrent to safeguard against an over-reaching government. If you are a gun owner you will have probably noticed that finding ammunition is not as easy as it once was. Why do you think this is happening? The founding fathers should have addressed ammunition in the founding documents. I believe that the federal government will attempt to render firearms useless by making ammunition scarce.

Every law abiding American ought to be well-armed; why should the criminals be the only one with the guns? The liberals want gun control, but that will only limit gun access to law abiding citizens. Do you think your neighborhood bank robber is registering his firearms? John Wayne said it best, "Life is hard, harder if you're stupid! (Wayne and Stryker 1949)" Don't be stupid, get a gun and fresh ammo and keep them close.

President Obama is the most radical president in the history of this nation. The thought of him winning a second term in office should have been absolutely horrifying. What political concerns exist for a second term U.S. President? <u>None</u>. We will see the real Barack Obama, yes, even more radical than his first four years as president. He does not believe in the rule of law and he has demonstrated that he does not respect the U. S. Constitution to which he took an oath to protect and defend. Apparently if he can't manipulate Congress into doing his bidding he will attempt to rule by executive order.

Much of conservative white America is afraid to call it for what it is for fear of being labeled racist. I'm black and the reason I don't like Obama is because his policies are not good for America. His belief that the government knows better and can take better care of us than we can take care of ourselves is exactly what we should expect from an individual with a socialist mindset.

It will be no surprise to me to see President Obama attempt to change or circumvent the 22nd Amendment to the United States Constitution to seek additional terms in office. I hope the country does not fall for this and therefore, establish an "American Monarchy".

Chapter 11

GOVERNMENT OVER-REACH

"My reading of history convinces me that most bad government results from too much government (Jefferson, Home › Jefferson › Quotations › Famous Quotations n.d.)." – Thomas Jefferson

NDAA

If you're not familiar with the National Defense Authorization Act (NDAA) legislation it should scare the hell out of you and every American. The NDAA has provisions that allow for the government to accuse any American of being a terrorist and therefore arrest and incarcerate for an unlimited period without trial. It also has provisions that would allow martial law here in America. Now what should scare us all is that this can't be blamed solely on the Democrats, as this was legislation that was supported by Republican lawmakers.

TSA

The Transportation Security Administration (TSA) occupies every major airport in the country. Now I have no desire to see another 9/11 and there are plenty of things we can do without violating the rights of American travelers to make air travel safe. The full body scans are offensive. These machines provide a virtual snapshot of the most personal parts of your body. Many Americans have been subjected to the pat downs or "frisks" and allegations of sexual assault have been made, yet no law enforcement agency in this country has ever investigated these allegations. Why, you ask? I will tell you why and that is because most County Sheriffs will not uphold their constitutional duties to act against any enemy foreign or domestic. I would be steadfast in responding to any allegation of criminal wrongdoing, yes, even against a federal agent as Sheriff. We must stand up and if you can't stand tall at least stand up!

There is a story told that if you drop a frog into a pot of boiling water the frog will jump immediately out. But if you drop that same frog into a pot of cold water and slowly bring it to a boil that frog will boil to death. This is what is happening in America. The slow disintegration of our liberty and freedom is not abrupt enough to make the masses jump out of the pot. So as patriots we must sound the alarm to either turn off the heat or get out of the pot.

We are all to blame for these things! We have allowed elected officials, both Democrat and Republicans alike, to tell us the same lies every two, four or six years and we keep voting them back into office. **I am still bound by that oath I took more than thirty years ago as a young Marine; "To protect and defend the Constitution of the United States of America against all enemies, foreign and domestic." This oath will live with me as long as I draw breath and I will never participate or obey any action to deny an American** citizen their rights as guaranteed by the Constitution. <u>**Why do we continue to allow so many elected leaders to vacate their oaths without serious consequences?**</u>

Barack Obama continues to be the most radical president ever to occupy the White House and should be brought up on impeachment charges. Obama has refused to uphold his oath to protect and defend the constitution, in fact he has openly violated it with his illegal alien policy, but Congress won't act to bring articles of impeachment. His behavior is a clear and present danger to the safety and security of these United States. On most every occasion when Republicans have questioned his performance; racism has been alleged. There may be some who will never like Obama because of his race. I for one don't like Obama because he has led the country to a place where it does not need to be. His fiscal policy has placed the United States on the verge of financial collapse and any Republican who goes along with any of his radical plans to continue raising the debt ceiling should be run out of the Party. There may be some things we can negotiate, but the accumulation of this crushing debt should not be one of them.

Remember President Obama's open microphone moment on March of 2012 while he was meeting with Russian President Dmitry Medvedev in Seoul, South Korea on the issues of European Missile Defense System? An open microphone captured Obama making this statement: "Let me get re-elected first, then I'll have a better chance of making something happen." "This is my last election, after my election, I will have more flexibility (Spetalnick and Holland 2012)."

I'm confused how Obama can tell this to the President of Russia, but not the American people. Is he going to roll over to appease another foreign power? I anticipate that Obama will spend the last month of his presidency signing letters of pardon to protect all of his illegal activities carried out by others.

President Obama promised to fundamentally change America and many people automatically assumed this was something good for America. All change isn't good change! On January 20, 2009, Obama's Inauguration day the total national debt was $10,626,877,048,913.08 (The Debt to the Penny and Who Holds It 2014). As of March 11, 2014 Obama had augmented the national debt to $ 17,491,079,219,453.82. In 47 months, just less than one full term in the White House, Obama has orchestrated the addition of $6,864,202,170,540.74 to the nation's debt. Now let's put this into perspective; this President has been responsible for adding more than half of the debt that was incurred under the combined 43 previous administrations.

The Fiscal year 2012 federal budget enacted was 3.796 trillion dollars. That means if we spent **no** money and earmarked all government revenue towards paying off the budget it would take us roughly four and a half years to eliminate the debt. That can never happen, but it goes to show you the massive mess we are in.

This is further proof of why Obama should not have been allowed to occupy the White House for another term. It's about performance and his economic policy has fundamentally changed this country. I guess he's doing exactly what he promised.

The conservatives that I know are judging Obama on his performance as President, not his ethnicity. I could care less what race he is if he were performing well and living up to his oath of office. The ability for America to elect a black president was proven in 2008 and that says a lot for how far we have come. It is not unfortunate that Americans re-elected a black president in 2012, it's just unfortunate that it was Obama. Yes, there are some who will never like Obama because of his race but that is an infinitesimal percentage of voting Americans.

Isn't this what the civil rights movement and Dr. King worked so diligently to accomplish? Obama's ethnicity should not give him additional rights or additional burdens. There are some who will never be happy with a minority in the white house and that's just the way it is. But I don't know how relevant the argument of racism can be carried forward as it relates to this president, because remember, Obama was first elected president in 2008, and re-elected in 2012.

Chapter 12

BLACK VS. AFRICAN AMERICAN

"We must learn to live together as brothers or perish together as fools (King, Jr. 2014)." – Dr. Martin Luther King, Jr.

Prior to the signing of the Emancipation Proclamation by President Lincoln in 1863 non-free blacks were called slaves and worse. Immediately after freedom they were referred to as former slaves, freed slaves, then Negros, Afro-American, and now African American. Well what's next? People of Pigmentation? **I consider myself to be an American who is black!** I am proud of my heritage and I am proud to be an American. In fact I have always been proud to be an American, unlike some. Michelle Obama voiced, after the 2008 election, that for the first time in her life she was proud of her country (Tapper 2008). Why was she finally proud, because enough people decided to elect her radical husband to the presidency? I don't need to tell you that what we're called is nowhere near as important as who we are. The man who threw that bottle at my sisters and I could not make us *"niggers"* by calling us the name. Remember Dr. King's, "Not the color of your skin, but the content of your character". But, Mrs. Obama, I will tell you that I am not proud that your husband is the President of the United States of America because he has weakened this country. **<u>The United States does not need a president of a particular color; it needs a president of a particular character!</u>**

Prior generations of Black and White Americans fought for us to be treated equally as free men and women. That is all that I want to be, free from tyranny, discrimination and made available to as much opportunity as possible. I am exactly who almighty God intended me to be, no more and no less. The stories of the Tuskegee Airmen (2011) and their desire to fight for this country always made me particularly proud. At the very time that these men were struggling for the right to fight for this nation in Europe, they were being denied the full rights as an American at home. Now, if this doesn't explain that special thing called being "American" then I don't know what does.

In my opinion with the exception of slavery, the United States of America was perfectly founded. It is time for all of us to live up to the sacrifices that were given for us by our American ancestors.

Chapter 13

TEA PARTY (TAXED ENOUGH ALREADY)

"Our constitution was made only for a moral and religious people. It is wholly inadequate to the government of any other (Adams n.d.)." – John Adams

The Tea Party movement has been one of the most important political movements in my lifetime. The Tea Party movement began in late 2008 and on April 15, 2009 at rallies across the country American Patriots gathered and called for a complete overhaul of government by accomplishing the following:

- Eliminate Excessive Taxes
- Eliminate the National Debt
- Eliminate Deficit Spending
- Protect Free Markets
- Abide by the Constitution of the United States
- Promote Civic Responsibility
- Reduce the Overall Size of Government
- Believe in "We the People"

TEA Party (Taxed Enough Already)

- Avoid the Pitfalls of Politics
- Maintain Local Independence

Because the Tea Party movement defied the political establishment in both parties, they have come under constant attack. The relentless charges of racism by Democrats were frequently thrown at the Tea Party with little or no proof. But my personal experiences with Tea Party groups have disproved this allegation. In the Tea Party I have met some of the kindest, most caring, dedicated American patriots who have a sincere concern for the future of this great republic. It is interesting that my involvement in politics mirrored the arrival of the Tea Party movement and I am proud to know that there are patriots on watch of our country.

I met former Alaskan Governor Sarah Palin on Super Bowl Sunday in 2010. She was traveling with her daughter, Piper. I was part of the dignitary security detail for Texas Governor Rick Perry. Governor Palin was in Houston for a rally supporting Governor Rick Perry's re-election at the Berry Center in northwest Harris County, Texas. Sarah Palin became the darling of the Tea Party during her bid for Vice President on the 2008 Republican ticket with Presidential candidate, John McCain. Her simple, common sense approach to government was a natural fit with the Tea Party movement.

I saw something with Governor Palin that really made me respect her. Upon her arrival at the arena and while in the staging area she went to each and every arena worker in the staging area and shook their hand and introduced herself and her daughter. She accomplished this in an unrushed manner which gave me the impression that it was a sincere move. This was classy, and it was nice to see her take the time to acknowledge the regular people who make this country go.

Most Tea Party organizations do not endorse political candidates, but I hope this changes. Many of today's uninformed voters look to the Tea Party for guidance in choosing a candidate; this is where the Tea Party can continue to build its influence and ensure conservatives are elected.

But, beware of some of these groups identifying themselves as Tea Party but not adhering to the true ideals of the Tea Party movement. No group or endorsing organization should ever endorse without fully vetting and interviewing <u>all</u> potential candidates seeking their endorsement. A primary goal of the Tea Party was not to be bound by heavy handed political Party leaders wanting to take away the group's ability to do what they collectively felt was right.

Some elected officials had the audacity to openly speak against the Tea Party in the early days of the movement, but have now changed their tunes, by proclaiming they were "Tea Party before Tea Party was cool"! This includes some State Senators, State Representatives and County wide elected officials of which we are acquainted. It's okay to change your mind, just don't lie about it. Pay much more attention to what people do than to what they say!

During the Saddle-Up Texas Straw Poll in early 2012 I had the opportunity to meet Andrew Breitbart. Andrew was a great conservative voice and I believe there were some who were very concerned about what he was going to expose. Andrew and I kept in touch for the next few months until his untimely death. Many questions are still unanswered as to the true cause of his death and strangely enough the Los Angeles coroner who performed the autopsy mysteriously died, and according to some sources poisoning appears to the cause of death. Andrew was a great patriot and called things for what they were and I sure hope that didn't get him killed. I last spoke to him about three weeks before his death and he said he had something really big coming on Obama! We may never know what exactly that was.

Figure 13 Andrew Breitbart and Carl at
Saddle-Up Texas Straw Poll January 2012

Chapter 14

THE CONSERVATIVE VOICES

"The Constitution is not an instrument for the government to restrain the people; it is an instrument for the people to restrain the government (Henry n.d.)."–Patrick Henry

For love of country, that's why they stand up and shout so we don't ignore the tide rolling in against freedom. If you are willing to stand up and speak against wrongdoing you will most certainly come under attack. If you talk for a living from time to time you will misspeak and that's okay. Just clarify yourself and move on and try not to do it again. **News Flash**, every time a liberal is called out, it's not racism. Every time Obama is criticized for his socialist actions it's not racism.

Sean Hannity:	Conservative radio and television talk show host
Rush Limbaugh:	Conservative radio and television talk show host
Glenn Beck:	Conservative radio host

Sarah Palin:	Former Governor of Alaska, from 2006 to 2009.
	2008 Vice-Presidential running mate w/ McCain
Allen West:	Former Lt. Colonel U.S. Army & Former Congressman for
	Florida's 22nd District
Sam Malone:	Conservative Radio, Television and Social Media Host.
	(AM1070 "The Answer") Houston, Texas

Sometimes the truth hurts; in this case I hope it serves as a serious wake up call. If we could not defeat Barack Obama with unemployment numbers above 8%, a completely failed economic policy, "Fast and Furious" and "Obamacare" then I think we have a problem. We failed to lead by convincing those who could be convinced, and changing the minds of those who otherwise didn't believe the facts. The mistake of venturing into areas in which a reasonable claim of racism could be used is harmful to our mission. The Republican Party is not a racist organization; however, that doesn't mean that there aren't some racists in the Party. It would be absolutely insane to believe that racism doesn't exist in the Party, because it sure seems to exist everywhere else. We have to police ourselves and not give any fuel for the liberal led media to attack us.

On April 18, 2011 an Orange County, California GOP member, Marilyn Davenport sent out a photograph with Obama's face on a young chimpanzee with two adult primates suggesting this was why Obama had not produced a birth certificate (see below). I don't know Ms. Davenport so I am not going to label her as a racist, but this type of behavior is extremely harmful and serves to shore up claims made by some Democrats that Republicans are racist. Davenport later apologized and claimed that this was political satire. But this is the type of behavior that Republicans cannot get involved in. It is the exact sort of distraction the Democrats wanted. How many "independents" and others saw this as racism, which led them to solidify their support against racism when the question they should have been left to answer was one about Obama's performance.

Figure 14 An example of destructive and negative media which does not serve Republicans well
(Photograph courtesy of www.change.org)

Chapter 15

RESPONSIBLE GROWTH OF THE GRAND OLD PARTY

"Insanity is doing the same thing, over and over again, but expecting different results (Einstein 2013)"
–Albert Einstein

I have been a conservative my whole life. Now trust me, I wasn't running around referring to myself as a conservative growing up in Fulshear, Texas in the late 60's and 70's, but the seeds were planted and over the years they took deep root. During my childhood I learned to work hard, be honest and respect others. I learned to respect and obey the law. I learned the importance of family and community. The importance of voting and civic involvement was never stressed to me. I don't think my mother ever cast a vote in her life. I didn't cast a vote until the 2010 primary. Voting was never stressed in my household as a child but I now know that every vote matters. I will not miss another opportunity to cast a ballot and my vote will always be given to the best <u>conservative</u> candidate. Is anyone surprised when a young man heads off to medical school when both of his parents are doctors? Can anyone be surprised that we have generations of Democrats that have no idea why they are Democrats? I am living proof that we are not confined to the place we start in life.

We can change most anything we put our minds to. An alcoholic doesn't stop drinking because he is loved by his family; alcoholics stop drinking when they first make up their own minds to quit and they admit that a problem exists. We must view many Democrats in this same way. I think many Democrats see the problems; we just have to step in and supply them with facts to make up their minds to change. I always knew I was conservative, but why was I drawn to the GOP? The GOP's goals to reduce the size of government, cut spending, reduce taxes, strengthen our military, being pro-life and supporting strong family values were key in my decision. But it was not because the GOP reached out to me. In comparison the Democrat Party's goals to further inflate the size of government, being pro-choice, military reduction, continuing entitlements was more than enough to be sure that I could never be a Democrat.

The GOP must quit assuming that all minorities, particularly Blacks and Latinos, are automatically Democrats. This assumption was used against me in my 2012 primary run for Sheriff and to some extent it worked. We must be willing to engage everyone that is like-minded because if we do not; I promise you the Democrats will. **We do not have to compromise our principles in order to grow the Party; but we must do a much better job of making our principles known.** There is no better time than now to encourage outreach, especially among the young. Don't show up in a minority community looking for support around election time unless you have planted roots in that community or you will look disingenuous.

We must take the conservative message into minority areas and accurately communicate the message. But we shouldn't go into those communities unless we are committed to staying there. We must communicate this to the younger generation of minorities and be willing to spend the time necessary so as not to appear as only being there for the vote and then leaving after the election. Good relationships are built and nurtured over time so trust can be established. You don't plant tomatoes a week before you want to eat them. You plant them early and you nurture and fertilize them so they grow healthy and strong. This is the same process that must go into building and adding to the conservative base.

Black Americans are a proud and God fearing people and a complete sharing of the facts are necessary to at least set the records straight. I believe that if this were done many young Blacks and Hispanics would naturally levitate towards the GOP. It defies belief that any Bible believing Christian could align with the Democrat Party for its stances on failing to protect the unborn and sanctioning same sex marriages.

Black conservatives have often been accused of being an "Uncle Tom". I don't know who Uncle Tom is, but I know we had all better keep a real close eye on Uncle Sam! Our ability as Republicans to responsibly grow the ranks is critical to our Party's survival. If a former Democrat wants to join the ranks then we must do our due diligence to make sure the "conversion" is genuine, but then welcome them in. Here is a good question for all of those who love to call others "RINO's". How long must a former Democrat be a Republican before they lose that title?

It is an undeniable truth that the majority of Black Americans vote Democrat because they have watched their parents and grandparents do so. Because of free flowing entitlements the Democrats have convinced many minorities that they have their best interest at heart and in the process generational curses have been put in place that have harmed generations of blacks in America. Many black households are father-less because government income requirements keep the fathers from living in the home. If not for these requirements some of these men would be present and responsible for their children.

Now this is the most disconcerting fact that I have encountered. Many blacks, even though they know that Barack Obama has not performed well, still voted for him. Why? Many older blacks believed that they would never see a black president in their lifetimes and they want him to have a full two terms in the office. That thinking is virtually impossible to change, trust me I have tried. That is why it is so important that each and every black conservative be identified and brought into the Republican Party and engaged to do more than just cast a GOP vote. Blacks must serve on committees within the Party and run and be elected to office. We must not only talk it, we must walk it. Proof by our actions is paramount!

I joined the Harris County (Houston, TX) Republican Party in early 2009 after the election of Barack Obama. I realized that **elections have consequences** and sitting silent for me, was no longer acceptable. In April of 2009 my grandson was born and I knew that the country was quickly heading downhill and I had to get involved. I decided to offer myself up as a candidate for Sheriff and put to use the skills that I had spent a lifetime acquiring.

I became a member of the Republican Leadership Council that same year. In early 2010 I was appointed to Chair the Committee on Law Enforcement for the county Party. I had not cast any vote anywhere until the 2010 Republican primary mid-term election. I made sure to share this with the Party Chair and to his credit he welcomed me into the Party.

I was later accused of being a Democrat plant because in 2008 I made a decision as an employee of the Harris County Sheriff's Office to support the Democrat nominee for the office against the Republican incumbent. My decision was based upon the fact that the Republican incumbent had failed to lead and was wrapped in scandal and controversy along with the Republican district attorney who had already been forced to resign from office.

I made that decision because I felt it was in the best interest of the agency and the public to get new leadership in place. Leadership requires making difficult decisions and replacing bad leadership shouldn't be a tough decision. I have never and will never let politics enter into my professional law enforcement decisions. Trust me – you do not want police officers making official decisions based upon their political ideologies.

After the election of the Democrat he quickly proved that his promises to lead the agency were completely undermined by his lack of management and leadership experience. That was in part my reason for running for the office in 2012.

The Hispanic Vote

There are some within the Republican Party who believe that we must cater to Hispanics for their vote. I believe that we must begin making ourselves attractive to all like-minded people. Some even believe that we must turn a blind eye to the U.S. and Mexican border in order to convince Hispanics that we are not anti-Hispanic. This reminds me of the affirmative action policies of the 1980's which allowed one wrong to exist in order to try and achieve another goal. We should not, as Republicans, be afraid to stand against something that is wrong. What do you think will happen if we continue to allow our country to be flooded with illegals? Well, I will tell you. The great cities of these United States will look like those not so great cities of third world countries. We will have cardboard cities, disease and crime problems on a magnitude that you cannot imagine. The argument has consistently been made that we cannot remove 11 million illegals from the United States. The cost and logistics of such an undertaking would be too extreme. Now is the time to deal with this issue because it's not getting any better. If we do not, what do you suppose we will do when the number hits 50 million or 100 million? Particularly when there are those who want to allow illegals the "right" to vote. This makes about as much sense as letting prisoners sit on the parole board!

When I was a boy I heard it said that the Mexicans had pledged to take back this land without firing a shot. If we are going to let that happen then what did those proud Texans die for at the Alamo? What do you think will happen when the numbers of illegals allow them to dominate every election? I don't believe that fairness will be at the top of their list of priorities. Well, give that some thought and I think you might arrive at the conclusion that I have and it's not a scenario that I wish to see.

This is not an anti-Hispanic message. This is a pro-American message. I don't want to lose my country to anyone, from anywhere. This is a country of many cultures and that is fine, but we are allowing a problem to happen that will have catastrophic results. I know many Hispanics who are as bothered by the senseless immigration policies that are continuing to add legions of illegals to our already overburdened social system. We have those who have manipulated the system to scurry across the border to have "anchor babies". Anchor babies are children born in the United States to immigrant (illegal) parents, who by virtue of their birth on American soil are citizens. Because of the citizenship of the child, many believe the parents have a right to stay.

This may sound a bit prideful, but the good Lord blessed me to be born in the greatest state, in the greatest country in the world. I am grateful for that and I cannot blame anyone who wants to come here. But, I am not willing to risk our way of life for some "politically correct" idea that the United States should continue to be all things for all people. We must first take care of ourselves and then and only then can we worry about taking care of others.

Chapter 16

THE ATTACK

"A lie gets halfway around the world before the truth has a chance to get its pants on." (Churchill, Winston Churchill quotes n.d.)."–Sir Winston Churchill

In March of 2008 a personal attack was launched towards me and one of the most disappointing things about the attack was that it was launched through my employer. The Texas Government Code provides certain protections for peace officers and firefighters which are in place to protect them from vindictive and untrue accusations. One of the main protections afforded is that a complaint **shall not be accepted** against a peace officer unless the complaint is in writing; and is signed by the person making the complaint. That is, in effect, the same assurance that every person in this country would be afforded; the right to know who their accuser is and be able to face them.

An employee at the company that employed my wife had anonymously reported that I had assaulted my wife. Now strangely enough, this was the same woman (who just

The Attack

happened to be black) that a couple of years earlier made a derogatory statement regarding our marriage, due to the fact that my wife is Caucasian and I am black.

My wife was approached in the lobby of her company's corporate office by two Internal Affairs Investigators from the Harris County Sheriff's Office. Now my wife is not and has never been a law enforcement officer and unfortunately these two investigators took full advantage of that. The investigators recorded the interview and asked several times if I had ever assaulted her. Again and again the investigators were told "NO", but that was not good enough so they pressed her and scared her to the point that she recited to them the allegation for fear that she would be arrested. The administration of the Harris County Sheriff's Office at that time violated the law by refusing to accept a complaint that my wife attempted to file the next morning.

I had been previously married to my first wife from January 1990 until we divorced in April 2005. We were involved in a post-divorce civil lawsuit over hundreds of thousands of dollars. One of the same IAD investigators made contact with her, at a location in another state. She had made allegations of abuse during a therapy session after the divorce was final, during the civil lawsuit. To her credit, she has apologized to me after her statements became public. She was subsequently interviewed by a Houston Chronicle newspaper reporter in 2012 and admitted that she had spoken out of anger and her allegations were untrue. For anyone who has gone through a difficult divorce I don't have to tell you some of the things that can be said in anger.

I was interviewed by Internal Affairs and denied the allegations because they were false. I was ordered to take a polygraph examination or be terminated. I submitted to the order and took the polygraph examination. Immediately prior to the examination I was confronted by that same IAD Investigator in an attempt to aggravate me. The polygraph examiner during the examination paused the examination and mentioned that my blood pressure was off the chart. Well, I explained to him the confrontation outside his office and told him to continue with the examination because I had been ordered under threat of termination to take the polygraph exam. The polygraph examiner reported that he felt there was deception in my responses. I was given a Letter of Reprimand for the polygraph examination and that was the end of it, or so I thought. This polygraph examiner would later become a supporter of my campaign for Harris County Sheriff.

Polygraph examinations are not allowed as evidence in any court in the United States because they are deemed to be unreliable. Do you find it strange that allegations of such a serious nature were never criminally investigated? Administrative investigations at the Harris County Sheriff's Office, unfortunately, were not operated within the strict confines of the law. Some inexperienced or bad-intentioned investigators believe their job is to prove allegations. That is a dangerous mindset and completely improper. An administrative investigation should seek and report the facts. The facts and only the facts should be the determining factor in the outcome, not the opinion or bias of the investigator.

The audio recordings of both my former and current wife were leaked from the sheriff's office during the campaign and strangely enough no investigation was ever launched by the Democrat Sheriff to determine how official records that are normally not released were leaked. It normally takes a filed complaint against the Sheriff to the State Attorney General to gain compliance in obtaining these types of records.

The most important thing is that I have never and would never do such a thing. There were those who ran with this as far and as fast as possible. It didn't matter that the allegation was untrue. It only mattered that it existed in an official document and it could be used against my campaign.

I eventually made the run-off election from a field of eight candidates. I accomplished this without any of the three major slate endorsements in the county. I subsequently lost the run-off to the candidate who did everything in his power to use the untrue allegation to win the run-off and outspent me more than $3 to $1. My opponent even went so far as to accuse me of being an undercover Democrat.

That opponent who was self-described as an "ultra conservative" was soon exposed and found to be accepting money from SOB's (Sexually Oriented Businesses) that fall under the direct supervision of law enforcement. This candidate's campaign had either borrowed or been given hundreds of thousands of dollars by individual(s) with ties to "SOB's". This same "ultra conservative" candidate's campaign was funneled $25,000.00 from a Sexually Oriented Business through a local law enforcement labor organization and this information was reported by local television and print media just days before the election. This individual had been fired for official misconduct from the same Sheriff's office to which he was seeking to be elected. This same "ultra conservative" candidate was endorsed by some major Republican leaders who apparently felt that he was the type of Sheriff they wanted. I wonder if those endorser's opinions will matter to the masses in upcoming elections.

The result in the election of November 6, 2012 was that this candidate was thoroughly beaten by the incumbent Democrat. There were large numbers of Republican voters who crossed over and voted for the Democrat to keep this individual from gaining power, and many Republican voters chose not to vote in the race (under vote) and finally this candidate, because of some of his publicized beliefs about certain minorities, could garner no support from the other side of the political coin. In fact this candidate garnered the fewest number of votes of any countywide Republican candidate and has been blamed for negatively affecting the "straight ticket vote" for Republicans in Harris County.

Now it is very important to note that in the final days of the run-off election, key Harris County elected and former elected officials endorsed him knowing the extensive baggage he was carrying. In the days following the election these same elected and former elected officials have now turned on others within the Harris County Party to attack and blame for their support of a bad candidate.

For those of you who are not familiar with the city of Houston, located in Harris County, Texas, it is very diverse and a Democrat stronghold, yet the unincorporated area of Harris County remains conservative. Past elections have proven that the inner city Democrats will support a common sense conservative Republican candidate.

The Attack

The end result, in my opinion, is that we have a Democrat Sheriff in office today because a couple of key Republicans refused to accept a candidate who was going to enforce the law, would not be a puppet, and possibly because they were too resistant to some of the positive change needed in the Republican Party. But they had an excuse they could hide behind to do it. That's a sad, but very true commentary on a very small, but powerful and vocal few within Harris County, Texas Republican politics.

Chapter 17

THE PARTY OF LINCOLN AND REAGAN

"Thou shalt not speak ill of any fellow Republican."
(California Republican Party Gaylord Parkinson 1966)
– Gaylord Parkinson

Ronald Reagan was my Commander-in-Chief during my service as a United States Marine. Reagan made great decisions for this country as President. Reagan also revealed incredible leadership during his 1966 run for Governor of California when he proclaimed: "Thou shalt not speak ill of any fellow Republican." That's great advice and our Party would be wise to adopt this practice. Our decency cannot just be rhetoric; it must be on constant display and we should reject any candidate who cannot conduct themselves accordingly. How many attacks leveled by Republicans against Mitt Romney during the 2012 Republican Presidential debates were well set in the minds of independents before Romney became the Party nominee and how many of those attacks were gift wrapped and used by Obama in the general election? How many opposed Romney and now would gladly have him as president?

President Lincoln, by his own stubborn determination brought about one of the most important pieces of legislation for blacks in the 13th Amendment and again, he was a Republican. You would have to agree that his assassination on Good Friday, April 14, 1865 would most likely never have occurred if not for his stance on freeing the slaves.

Most Republican County parties sponsor a Lincoln and/or Reagan Day event. It is normally one of, if not the largest annual party sponsored events. I have often heard of the leadership of President Lincoln and President Reagan being a guiding light for the Party. But I see so much un-Lincoln/Reagan conduct within the Party. We must practice what we preach and start from within to build the Party to live up to being called the Party of Lincoln.

Chapter 18

REPUBLICAN WOMEN'S CLUBS (RWC)

"In politics, if you want anything said, ask a man. If you want anything done, ask a woman." (Thatcher 1965)
—Margaret Thatcher

The Republican Party gets things done because of its women. Much of my desire to stay involved and run for office again is because of the fine Republican women that I have gotten to know over these past years. The RWC members work countless hours without pay, but with the satisfaction of knowing their work matters. I would be remiss if I did not mention a couple of these groups by name here, from the greater Houston area. The Kingwood Area Republican Women, Village Republican Women, Tejas Republican Women, Memorial West Republican Women, The Daughters of Liberty and the Bay Area Republican Women were clubs that I became very familiar with during my run for Harris County Sheriff in 2012. From the monthly luncheon meetings to the ongoing fundraising efforts throughout the year these women walk the walk and talk the talk by using their time, talent and treasures to help elect Republican candidates.

I would be remiss to not thank the many other clubs, far too many to mention here, who welcomed me and made me feel like part of their family. Harris County is home to many Republican clubs; so many that one could visit a Republican club every night of the month and not come close to making it to all the club meetings. The great work these fine volunteers do is very much appreciated and I want to make sure that I thank ALL of them for not only their faithful work but also for welcoming my candidacy.

Every Republican candidate elected to office can, in major part, thank Republican women for their success. I can honestly say that it was an honor to know these hard working patriots. God bless the Republican Women and Thank you!

Chapter 19

PRIMARY VS. GENERAL ELECTION CANDIDATES

"Hell I never vote for anybody, I always vote against. (Taylor 1949) – W.C. Fields

In football you wouldn't be wise to pick a team based on how well they played the first half of football games. You have to pick the team who can close the deal. The 2012 Republican Presidential Primary was absolutely brutal for those candidates who entered the fray. I may be a bit biased, but I truly believe that if Rick Perry had performed well during those televised debates; he would have been the Republican nominee. As voters and as a Party we must support the candidates who can win the *general* election. Who cares about a primary winner if they're going to get defeated during the general election?

Republicans too often use the primary as a "bloodletting" instead of picking the candidate who has the best chance to win and then solidifying support behind that candidate.

I was once told that most voters select their candidate because they have found an emotional connection with the candidate. That means something important to the voter is also important to the candidate. Ask yourself what is most important to you; a conservative candidate that you agree with 80% of the time or the liberal democrat candidate that you most likely will never agree with. We must quit destroying our candidates thereby setting them up to lose to the liberals. Once we have chosen the best candidate we must all get behind them and push. Have you noticed the Democrats don't seem to attack their own as we Republicans seem to? You may never hear me say this again, but maybe we need to take that out of their playbook.

I sincerely hoped that Mitt Romney would be the next President of the United States and I did my part to support him even though he was not my first choice. God knows this country is strong, but I don't know if we can survive a second term of Barack Obama.

Chapter 20

RACISM – DOES IT EXIST IN THE GOP?

"Racism is a refuge for the ignorant. It seeks to divide and to destroy. It is the enemy of freedom, and deserves to be met head-on and stamped out." (Berton n.d.) Pierre Berton

Racism exists in the Republican Party just as it does in the Democratic Party. It has not been my experience that it is anything but the narrow minded beliefs of a small few, and I will not disrespect the vast majority of fine, hardworking, fair-minded Republicans who are only interested in electing the most qualified, service-minded candidates. An unwarranted racism allegation is a hateful and harmful thing particularly when there is no evidence to support it. It is called, "Playing the Race Card". I learned long ago to look in the mirror when you encounter a problem and check yourself before accusing anyone else. But when and if there is racism discovered in the GOP it should not be hidden, but publicly dealt with and discouraged regardless of who has harbored it.

The fear of being accused of racism cannot and should not stop conservatives from standing firm against the things we know to be wrong.

First let me tell you where I am coming from. I do not believe in affirmative action. The idea of giving one person an unfair advantage over another is exactly what the civil rights movement attempted to correct. Remember Mama's advice... "What's right is right and what's wrong is wrong, no matter who does it."

One of the questions most frequently asked of me during my campaign for Sheriff was what it was like being a black conservative. I would joke sometimes and say it doesn't hurt because I take medication for it, but with Obamacare I might not be able to afford it. Seriously, there are many conservatives of all ethnicities. The best move the Republican Party can make is to embrace all like-minded individuals that share our values regardless of ethnicity. We as a party must quit assuming that all blacks will vote Democrat and start having conversations on the "other side of the tracks". The Republican Party cannot just expect minorities to join up, vote and sit silent. Minorities will and should run for office and should be judged on their abilities just as any other candidate.

In early 2010 I attended a fundraiser for a local Republican State Representative. This event was in the club house of a gated and exclusive community in Fort Bend County, Texas (a suburb of Houston). At one point during the evening I was being introduced throughout the room by a dear friend. She introduced me several times by saying, "This is Carl Pittman, and he's a black conservative Republican running for Sheriff in Harris County." Now I could hear the pride in her voice that she was introducing a "black" conservative Republican. She did this a couple more times when I laughed and said to her, "You know if you just introduce me as a conservative Republican running for Sheriff of Harris County, they'll figure out that I'm black." This got quite a chuckle. The truth is there are many black conservatives; the mission must be to locate, identify and welcome them into the Party. I know plenty of black conservatives, but until they are made to feel welcome into the folds they will stay on the exterior and that doesn't serve us well.

Our mission as Republicans and Conservatives must be to grow our ranks. In doing this we can move the Party forward and save this great place that we call America.

Chapter 21

ELECTED OFFICIALS

"Politics, it seems to me, for years, or all too long, has been concerned with right or left instead of right or wrong. " (Armour 2013) – Richard Armour

Do you think power corrupts? The old adage "Power corrupts, absolute power corrupts absolutely" has certainly been exemplified by the Obama administration. This isn't simply a Democrat or Republican problem; it's an unfortunate part of politics. I believe that most people enter politics with good intentions to make things better and when we find a true public servant we must support them because they will come under attack. With great power comes great responsibility, to steal a phrase from Superman. The founding fathers envisioned the "Citizen Statesman" as an individual who would step forward to serve and at the end of their term; go home and let another lead.

Government has become ineffective because of the "deal making" career politicians Career politicians get elected and re-elected again and again and that's the fault of us as voters.

If you are fortunate enough to be represented by good people then do all you can to keep them in office as long as they continue to represent your interest. I don't think term limits in most cases serve the best interest of the people. It is hard to believe that business or government can be accomplished without some compromise. Governing can be accomplished without compromising your principles.

During my run for Sheriff a certain high ranking elected official worked very diligently to derail my campaign. Now I'm not talking about a city council member, I mean a state level official with some very lofty political goals of his own. This man spent most of the 2012 primary season backing a long entrenched establishment candidate who he just a few years earlier was calling names on the radio. Now what's interesting about this is that I barely knew him. He threatened one of his own employees with their job if they volunteered to help during the event when Sheriff Arpaio came to Houston in support of my campaign.

There is nothing wrong with supporting the candidate of your choice; in fact that is what each and every one of us should do. But when elected officials start bullying people using their political office and influence they need to be forced to answer, "Why?"

Chapter 22

THE MEDIA

"All I know is just what I read in the papers, and that's an alibi for my ignorance." (Rogers 1923)–Will Rogers

The First Amendment to the U. S. Constitution protects our freedom of speech and that freedom is very important to keep us informed as to the workings of our government. In 1920 future President Franklin D. Roosevelt was stricken with polio and subsequently was confined to a wheelchair. Most all of the Washington media was aware of that fact, but it was never reported on to the public. The country was much different because then; even the media recognized that protecting the office of the presidency was more important than the world knowing that Roosevelt was physically impaired. Do you think the world would have viewed America as weak or strong if the president was constantly seen in a wheelchair?

The American media reports the news as in such a way, that if the country failed they will somehow continue. Can you imagine the press sitting on a similar story today? The problem with the liberal press today is that they will not report on certain issues and will routinely not report the truth. Has any president in recent history been more "protected" by the media than Barack Obama? Scandal after scandal has gone under-reported or completely ignored; the "Fast & Furious" operation, the Benghazi attack, and the IRS Tea Party scandal to name just a few.

I have read that public enlightenment is the forerunner of justice and the very foundation of democracy. The goal of the press should be to further those ends by seeking the truth and providing fair accounts of the issues. Physicians are bound by the Hippocratic Oath which has them swear to uphold a number of professional and ethical standards. Unfortunately, there is no such oath for journalists or their editors. I believe that most journalists sincerely want to operate in an ethical manner, but the problem is that each must decide their own standards and that can be problematic.

A former Houston area investigative reporter was despised by many current and former public officials because of his hard hitting investigative reports on corruption. If public officials would only do their duty investigative reporters would have very little to do. Integrity is doing the right thing when no one is looking; if your integrity is lacking, then assume someone is watching.

How We Hold The Media Accountable

How often have you asked yourself over the last four years, "Why doesn't the media report the facts regarding President Obama?" I think it's fair to say that FOX does a great job of reporting the facts against Obama, but CBS, NBC, CNN, and ABC are lacking in their reporting when it comes to the Obama Administration.

Television is driven by advertising dollars. If the big three, ABC, CBS and NBC, want to continue to ignore Obama's antics then here is what I suggest we conservatives should do. Let's hit their advertisers in the pocket. Let's pick the biggest advertiser and boycott that company's product for 30 days if they advertise on a network that refuses to report the "whole story". The point is not to put the company out of business, but to demand that it not spend their advertising dollars with a network that will harm their consumers and we should demand fair news reporting. You get the point. <u>Corporate America listens to one thing, and that is profits!</u>

I became a bigger fan of Chic-Fil-A when the leadership of that privately held corporation stood up against the moral decay of this country by speaking out against homosexuality. The liberal media did their best to make a story that would injure this company, but what did like-minded Americans do? They spent their money at Chic-Fil-A and for many weeks the lines at Chic-Fil-A were incredible. Chic-Fil-A undoubtedly set revenue records by doing the right thing.

During the halftime of an NFL football game during the 2012 season, NBC Sports announcer Bob Costas decided to use his position to attack the 2nd Amendment of the U.S. Constitution. A few days earlier a Kansas City Chiefs football player had fatally shot and killed his girlfriend who was also the mother of his three year old daughter. The player then went to the Chiefs training facility, and in the presence of his head coach and a few others turned the weapon on himself and committed suicide. This was a tragic incident which left a three month old little girl with no mother or father.

Bob Costas, in true liberal fashion, on live television, reasoned that the tragedy would not and could not have occurred if there were no guns. Moments after viewing this I took to Facebook and shared what I had just witnessed and 100% of the responses to my post thought that Costas, using a network broadcast of a sporting event to spread his liberal anti-second amendment rhetoric was wrong. Over the next several days social media was buzzing about Costas' attack on the 2nd Amendment. However, NBC felt this was appropriate and took no action against Costas.

Here are the facts: I have been around weapons all my life, as a country boy out hunting, as a combat trained United States Marine and a veteran professional law enforcement officer. Professional golfer, Nick Price once said that in all his years of playing golf he had never seen the hole come to the ball. There is one thing that I have never seen and that is firearm harm anything or anyone without some outside human assistance. If there is not a gun around then a knife or some other weapon will be used. The issue is an evil heart!

Obama, in true liberal fashion, will take full advantage of this tragedy to push some misguided anti-gun legislation. But do you think Obama will order his Secret Service Agents to lock up their automatic weapons? Of course not, Obama believes that an unarmed America is a more easily controlled America. That thinking falls in line with why all socialist governments want to disarm their people. The 2nd Amendment gives you the right to protect yourself and I strongly support it. Don't be the one without the gun when something bad is happening!

Do liberals really think that taking guns away from law-abiding Americans is the solution? That would only lead to the

The Media

CRIMINALS being the only ones armed. I love my country; I would die for it! I love my family; I would die for them! But I'm not going to die without one hell of a fight and my guns are going to be there with me. There are too many instances around the country that have proven if one gun packing true blue American had been armed many lives could have been saved. Have you ever stopped to ask yourself why these tragedies keep happening in areas where guns are "not allowed"? Gun safe zones such as schools don't deter the bad guys from carrying guns! That's because bad guys don't follow the law. Good guys with guns deter bad guys with guns!

There is no way to legislate evil out of the human heart. God gave man domain over everything on this earth and along with that authority came free will and sometimes people will do unspeakable things to one another. The best that we can do to mitigate those unspeakable things is to be prepared to deal with them when they happen.

The bad guys like to hunt where there is an unarmed target-rich environment and no one shooting back. (New Town, CT.) Sandy Hook Elementary School shooting is the perfect example of what happens when you have a gun free zone. Had there been a good guy with a gun there, I believe the outcome would have been much different.

Chapter 23

THE VALUE OF LIFE

"A baby is God's opinion that the world should go on. (Sandburg n.d.)" – Carl Sandburg

First of all let's call it what it is. **It is MURDER!** You abort a take-off or landing in an airplane, not a baby! It is my belief that life starts at conception. The law in many states will charge an individual with two counts of murder if that individual kills a pregnant woman, and rightfully so. But by some strange phenomenon that same pregnant woman can murder that same baby through abortion without any legal consequence. **Pro-choice should be what is exercised before there is a pregnancy. Either have no sex, safe sex or live with the consequences of sex.**

In 1973 the U.S. Supreme Court in a 7-2 decision established in Roe v. Wade (ROE V. WADE 1973)(Roe v. Wade, 410 U.S. 113 (1973). The right for women to murder babies through abortion. This is and always will be an immoral decision. Life is created and is the sole province of God.

The Value of Life

The Ten Commandments are commonly misquoted by saying, "Thou shall not kill". The actual commandment states and mandates, "Thou shall not murder." The execution of a convicted person is not murder and does not violate God's law. So for anyone wanting to argue the anti-death penalty angle, keep looking! The death penalty is 100% effective in eliminating recidivism!

It has baffled me for years that so many black pastors can support and vote Democrat. The vast majority of black pastors will tell you that they are Democrats, but cannot reconcile why they support a Party that sanctions the right of women to murder their unborn children. I have put that question to several black ministers and have yet to receive an answer that explains how biblically, they can support the Democrat platform which sanctions the murder of babies.

An unplanned pregnancy can surely present some challenges, but make no mistake the murder of an innocent child cannot and should not be an option.

According to the Guttmacher Institute there were 1.21 million abortions performed in the United States in 2008 which is an average of 3,322 murders per day (Guttmacher Institute 2013), 138.4 every hour, 2.31 abortions every minute of every day. The current concern in this country is falling off the fiscal cliff. We have already fallen off the moral cliff.

On December 14, 2012 in Newtown, Connecticut an armed man entered Sandy Hook Elementary School and murdered twenty-six (26) people including twenty (20) first graders. This event was horrific and as a father I truly hope that God never calls upon me to bury one of my children. This incident was carried as the lead story on every news outlet in the country for several days following. This tragedy was carried out by an evil and/or disturbed mind who, in the aftermath took his own life. This has led many liberals and others to call for snap response gun control laws. No law will ever be written that will contain the evil in the heart of a human being. If almighty God's law is violated every day then what makes anyone believe that a law written by man will remedy evil?

Now not to make light of the Newtown tragedy, but the single day murder of 20 children hardly compares to the murder of 3,322 children every day in this country and you will rarely if ever see a news report on the slaughter of the thousands of babies each and every day.

Chapter 24

BLOGGERS

"A lie will travel around the world before the truth gets its boots on. (Churchill, "True Origin Unknown" Winter 2009-2010)" **– Sir Winston Churchill**

The internet and social media have given rise to blogs. Blogs are everywhere and provide an avenue for the regular person to create a forum to discuss issues, promote ideas or distort facts or even flat out lie. Whenever a person hides behind a screen name I just can't take their opinion too seriously. If you have something to say; stand up and say it. Blogs have created the perfect playground for the "virtual bully". I know a few political bloggers and for the most part they are decent people who sincerely care about their country and communities. I will discuss two in particular because they each possess a keen ability to distort the facts. I will refer to them as Blogger #1 – "Little Grumpy" and Blogger #2 – "The Bankrupt Blogger"

Little Grumpy and I sat for lunch during the early stages of my campaign for Harris County Sheriff. Now mind you I had been warned that he would distort facts, but I felt it was only fair not to pass judgment until I got to know him. I guess a clue was, if you take a look at his blog page where it states that his blog is his "Attempt to tell the truth." How do you attempt to tell the truth? You either tell the truth or you don't. We sat for a couple of hours and discussed everything from politics to business. I left feeling as though nothing discussed could possibly be misinterpreted. Little Grumpy and I would run into each other from time to time over the next year and I began to feel like he was okay. I guess that was because nothing bad had happened, yet.

The initial primary election came and went. I made it into a run-off from an eight person field. I had been endorsed by six of the seven Senatorial District Chairmen in the Houston, TX area, the vast majority of the State Republican Executive Committee Members and an overwhelming number of precinct chairmen. My opponent had outspent me 3 to 1 and most of his money was loaned or given to him by a questionable source with ties to the sex industry, but that didn't matter to Little Grumpy. Little Grumpy went on a full unprovoked attack using the unfounded IAD investigation because he had decided to support my opponent and he wanted to make sure I did not win. In fact he completely disregards facts that proved the allegations against me were false.

The Bankrupt Blogger was truly a strange bird. He decided early in the campaign season to appear at almost every campaign event and did his best to befriend me. There was something about the man that made me feel uneasy. He reportedly had suffered through bankruptcy at some point in his past and was angry at the world. He had reportedly been kicked off of other Republican campaigns because he did not work well with others. My years in law enforcement had honed my skills to detect deceptive characteristics. He would audio record every event, but never post any of the recordings. This was obviously because there was nothing he could do to "doctor up" the footage. His attacks were filled with anger and he seemed intent on trying to personally destroy me, but I'm still here and I won't stop. I have prayed for both of these men and forgiven them.

Bloggers, be truthful in what you write! Your credibility will last as long you allow it to. Don't abuse your first amendment right because others died so you could have that right. But ultimately, God bless you both just be fair and accurate in your reports if you want anyone to take you seriously.

Chapter 25

CORRUPTION IN GOVERNMENT AND POLITICS

"When they call the roll in the Senate, Senators do not know whether to answer "Present" or "Not Guilty". (Roosevelt n.d.)–Theodore Roosevelt

The power and influence of elected office has been the draw to many that enter politics. Countless numbers of individuals have been elected for offices ranging from your local city council to national offices who quite honestly want the position for personal gain. In 2012 a local Democrat in Harris County, Texas (Houston) for District Attorney admitted that he only ran for the office for the name recognition it would give, in order to help his law practice, and amazingly he won his Party primary. Thankfully, the voters did not elect him into office. Would you be surprised to find that the vast majority of these individuals have their personal wealth continue to grow as they "serve"? This wealth doesn't appear to be a result of them saving their government paychecks. Many somehow manage to consult on projects that, in any other business would be considered a conflict of interest, but it seems as though somehow if you are in certain elected positions the rules don't apply to you.

A study done by the Center for Responsive Politics revealed that congressional members' personal wealth collectively increased by more than 16% between 2008 & 2009 (Center for Responsive Politics n.d.). While the overall portfolios of a few members lost value, don't worry, they are doing just fine.

Consider these facts:

Two hundred and sixty-one (261), or almost half of the members of congress are millionaires – now compare that to the fact that 1% of Americans are millionaires. (Center for Responsive Politics n.d.) Of these congressional millionaires, 55 had a calculated wealth of ten million ($10,000,000.00) or more! Now sit down for this one; eight had a calculated wealth of one hundred million ($100,000,000.00) (Center for Responsive Politics n.d.).

You might ask yourself how any of these federal lawmakers can relate to what most Americans deal with on a daily basis? Most have no worry about unemployment, foreclosures, and healthcare and even on the rare occasions they are removed from office for wrongdoing, they have nothing to worry about as their pensions are safe, because they wrote the laws to protect themselves. Most members of Congress rank among the wealthiest Americans, a goal that is all but unattainable by most of those they represent. Now it is not my intention to completely enrage you, well maybe it is, but what job in America can you work for only two years, get fired, and then receive a lifetime pension? That would be the U. S. Congress.

In 2009, the median wealth of a U.S. House member was $756,010.00, up from $645,503.00 in 2008. The median wealth of a U.S. Senator was nearly 2.38 million, up from 2.27 million in 2008 (Center for Responsive Politics n.d.). The average member of Congress is eight times wealthier than the median U. S. family in 2009. The average U. S. Senator was nearly twenty-five times wealthier than the median U. S. family in 2009 (Center for Responsive Politics n.d.).

Are you starting to get a sense of why these folks are so interested in staying in office? It is not in our best interest to continue to elect people to offices who have little or no idea of the struggles that most Americans face every day.

God bless them for making money, but these sorts of increases in wealth beg the question for whom are they looking out? I don't think they are looking out for us!

America's founding fathers envisioned "Patriot Statesmen", individuals that would be elected and serve then return home, thus allowing another individual to serve. But today we have those who believe they have a "right" to hold certain offices indefinitely or get themselves on the political staircase. They will move from one office to the next, using their political clout to move up and destroy anyone who attempts to run against them. They will use their influence to get appointments to key positions for their friends and family. Is that why you elected them or did you want them to **look out for you and your interests**?

Political Bullies

In recent years there seems to have been an uptick in episodes of bullying reported amongst school-aged children.

In some of these cases children have committed suicide when they felt they could no longer handle the pressure. Well it's going on in politics as well. I think every one of us has the right to support the candidate or issue of our choice. I may not agree with your choice, you may not agree with mine, but neither of us has the right to attack the other because of it. If I disagree with you then I may try my best to convince you to see it my way, but in the end, if you don't agree with me that has to be okay.

Elected officials who use their offices to appoint or endorse their friends are unfortunate. There are even some elected officials who have used their political power to threaten individuals for the endorsement choices they have made. Many of the bad behaviors that elected officials exhibit can be corrected if voters quit making excuses for bad conduct. The end result of it all is damaging to our country and if we want to turn the ship around and get on a good course we have to hold everyone elected to office fully accountable.

Be careful of these high level endorsements that so often have nothing to do with what is in our best interest.

The Morning After

Too many Republicans take the primary to be the opportunity to cannibalize other Republicans while losing sight of the goal, which is to win the general election. You will see some of the most vile and vicious attacks imaginable. Candidates will have their integrity, loyalty and families attacked. But then something very strange happens the morning after the primary election. Let's all be friends again! This is the most idiotic charade I have ever witnessed. How can you possibly hate someone and call them all sorts of vile things and then not understand why they might not ever want to associate with you again? How about the candidates in a race who will destroy one another, but then play the "we're all Republican" game when it comes to the general election.

I'm sorry, but a bad person and a bad candidate remain "BAD" regardless of the date on the calendar. The primary should be the period to vet candidates and find the candidate who can not only best represent you, the voter, but ultimately the candidate who can win the general election.

Truth in Politics……………………..Seriously!

Before the 2010 mid-term elections here in Texas many Republican State Representatives were under significant pressure from their constituents to not vote to re-elect Joe Strauss as House Speaker. Speaker Strauss was under attack by conservative Republicans for several issues, appointing Democrats as committee chairs, accepting campaign funds from pro-choice groups, etc.

Now whether or not you like or even know Joe Strauss is not the story. I have met and spoken with Speaker Strauss on a couple of occasions and all I can tell you is he seemed like a very decent man to me, but as a conservative I'm not thrilled with the way in which he has led as House Speaker. The story here is the posturing done by State Representatives who were under a great deal of pressure from their constituents to not support Strauss for Speaker.

Texas District 28 State Representative John Zerwas, during several public appearances made it very clear that he was in support of Speaker Strauss and would be continuing that support by voting for him to continue as Speaker. Zerwas, during a public meeting at a Fort Bend County, Texas library, was put under tremendous pressure to change his mind. Zerwas impressed me with the fact that he was willing to publicly discuss his decision and had the conviction to do what he felt was right. There was no surprise when John Zerwas cast his vote in support of Joe Strauss for Speaker. More importantly his constituents knew exactly what to expect.

Do you see the pattern here? Voters must hold elected officials accountable or stop complaining about the quality of leadership provided!

How many "conservatives", if they were put on trial could be convicted of being conservative? Is there enough evidence to convict you?

The simple test is to require specific details from those you support. That means you have to show up and ask them very direct questions. Record the conversations and do it openly. If they keep their word then continue your support of them. I do not fully support term limits because in the event that a public servant comes along and does exactly what they promise, they should have our continued support. If they don't; do everything you can as a voter to "un-elect" them. We must collectively start to look out for our own interest and we can do this effectively by ridding ourselves of ineffective, dishonest, self- serving politicians.

Why Obama Won Re-Election

It is important to note that Obama never shut his campaign machine down in 2008. So for four years while many

Republicans were fooled and in a euphoric state after the 2010 midterm election the Democrats were preparing for 2012. I spoke earlier of those who think winning the first half of a football game is the goal when the score after the fourth quarter is all that matters. But first let's look at the election results from Tuesday, November 6, 2012.

Popular Vote: **Electoral Vote:**
                                              (270 needed to win)

Obama – 64,694,882 ...50.8% (Politico Staff 2013)   332
Romney – 60,394,763...47.4%   206

In the weeks after the election many reasons have been given as to why Obama won re-election. We must study this election for several reasons. First we do not want to see this happen again and we had better learn something from this. But more importantly we had better study why Romney lost.

1. **FEAR** – Mitt Romney lost this election on the stage during those seemingly endless Republican debates. Do you not think that the Democrats were looking and listening to the attacks our Republican candidates were launching at each other? Mitt Romney was not my first or even second choice to be the nominee, but attacks not related to the issues of the presidency should never have been launched at any of the candidates. The issues in my mind are Constitutional ideology, economic policy, monetary policy, foreign policy, energy policy and the military. These issues are the very foundation of this country's strength. These are and will continue to be the issues that presidential candidates should have to

be prepared to answer. In the aftermath of the election those attacking Romney for his Mormon faith should have asked themselves if they were more aligned with Romney's faith or the confessed Islamic religious links that Obama brought to the office.

2. **LATINOS** – have become the "target" audience for both parties. Latinos are hard-working, pro-life, and pro-family people with strong Christian-based beliefs. Did anyone notice that Obama, in a last minute effort to sway younger Latinos, issued an executive order for federal immigration officials to effectively disregard the law when it came to certain Latino groups? Why do you think this was done in 2012 and not in 2009? We must welcome those Latinos who share our conservative values, but we cannot be afraid to speak out on issues of illegal immigration for fear of alienating some potential Latino voters. This is a country of laws and anyone wanting to share in it must be first willing to obey the law. Let's quit letting the comment of "They are hardworking, law abiding people" go unchecked. Their very presence is in violation of the law.

3. **Women** – the pro-choice vs. pro-life issue and equality for women in the work place. Romney, in my opinion made a Republican primary decision and knew he had to come out definitively pro-life to win the Republican nomination. This is purely a religious question for me and I believe that abortion is wrong and to kill an innocent child is a violation of God's law. This is however, a difficult question for many in the case of rape and/or incest. I believe that we as Republicans should not

vacate our values to chase votes. The "Binders full of women" quote was used to paint Romney as insensitive to the needs of women. Has anyone considered the fact that Obama's radical Islamic connections still see women as property? Take a look at Sharia Law. If that doesn't scare all of us, especially women, nothing will. Equal pay and benefits should be given to anyone who does the work.

4. **Elderly & Retired Voters** – the belief that Romney/Ryan would eliminate Social Security and its related benefits scared many senior voters. The Democrats effectively convinced many Americans that Social Security would be dismantled if Romney were victorious. This, for someone whose entire livelihood depended upon Social Security, was a terrifying prospect. Even though I believe many of these people liked what Romney brought to the table about jobs, business and other policies, they were thoroughly convinced by the Democrats that Romney was anti-them!

5. **Homosexuals and Lesbians** – In an obvious move to bring the Gay, Lesbian and Transgender support his way Obama **evolved** his thinking to support gay marriage. He relayed to America that his young daughters had somehow convinced him it was the right thing to do. I will first tell you that I do not condone the verbal or physical attack of anyone because of their orientation. However, again this is a religious question for me and my Holy Bible identifies the practice as an abomination (Lev. 18:22).

6. **Minority Voters (Specifically Blacks)** – During the 2012 election season I was amazed, but not surprised to see the number of black voters who publicly stated they were voting for Obama **regardless** of his performance, in fact they were voting for him solely because he was black. I can understand the pride of seeing for the first time in this country's history the election of a black president, but what I don't understand is how after watching his complete failure for four years that pride would "override" common sense and cause a second vote to be cast for him. I would not vote for or against someone based on the color of their skin. The presidency is about performance not pigmentation! Most blacks would not even consider publicly discussing the possibility of voting for Romney. The unemployment rate for blacks in November of 2012 was 13.2% (Data Brief: Black Employment and Unemployment December 2012 2013) while at the same time the national average for unemployment was 7.9%. I'm not sure I can make sense of why blacks would overwhelmingly support someone who has created fewer jobs for them than the rest of the population.

Chapter 26

THE CONVENIENT CONSERVATIVE

It's not hard to make decisions when you know what your values are. – Roy E. Disney

In the hot Texas heat of 1967 in the middle of cotton season I was just a young boy of four years of age. My two older sisters were already in elementary school. I wasn't feeling well one day and was too young to be left home alone. My mother knew that she had to go and pick cotton, but was faced with the dilemma of what to do with me. My mother never subscribed to leaving me home alone at that age, but at the same time knew that she had to go because the cotton farmers weren't too fond of having their crops in the field one day longer than was necessary.

Now for those of you, who have never picked cotton, let me begin by telling you that it is not a task for the weary or the weak. There were multiple cotton fields in the western part of Fort Bend County, Texas in Orchard, Texas to be exact. Cotton is planted in rows that seem to go on forever and the normal way to pick it at that time was to put a long cotton sack over your shoulder and get after it. The cotton sack was 12 to 15 feet long with a long shoulder harness. To pick cotton you were bent at the waist all day to reach the crop. Cotton blooms from very tough bulbs and using your bare hand you pull the cotton fiber from the bulb and place the cotton fiber in the sack. The bulbs were very unforgiving on the hands and bloody fingers were a normal result. A day of picking cotton would start early in the morning and conclude just before sundown. I can remember my mother picking four to five hundred pounds of cotton in a single day and earning 15 to 20 cents per pound. Dragging that heavy cotton sack up and down those long rows in the blistering Texas heat was not fun, but was very necessary if you wanted to earn a living during cotton season.

Now on this particular day my mother made a decision to take me with her to the cotton fields. Being protective as she was she did not feel safe leaving me laying under the cotton trailer to shield me from the sun for fear of a snake biting me or be my being run over if the cotton trailer was moved. So my mother made a decision that quite frankly I have never and will never forget. She had me lay on her cotton sack and she placed a large straw hat on me to shield me from the sun and she pulled me up and down those long rows picking cotton the entire day. I probably weighed 45 pounds or so my added weight on her cotton sack could not possibly have made the day easier on her. I don't remember how much cotton my mother picked that day, but she surely did what she had to do to ensure my safety and make a living. It wasn't the most convenient thing she could have done; in fact it was probably the toughest thing. This is the type of commitment to doing what is necessary that is missing from America today from parents to politicians.

Fast forward to the government shutdown of 2013 when the Republican controlled house was faced with taking the federal government into default for the first time in its history or letting Barack Obama plunge this nation into further debt by increasing the debt ceiling. Hundreds of thousands of federal employees had been furloughed and the liberal media was blaming Republicans for the entire thing. Ever wonder why there are so many federal employees, during the government shutdown of 2013 the Washington Examiner reported that according to Reuters 93% of the Environmental Protection Agency (EPA) had been furloughed and that only the essential personnel were still working. I think a great argument could be made that none of the employees of the EPA are essential. The EPA is as a regulation spewing, job killing federal agency run by another unelected bureaucrat. There are far too many of these bureaucrats in government. Over the years the federal government has missed the mark, the government has misplaced their true role which is to create an environment where business can thrive and private sector jobs will be created.

But back to the convenient conservatives that we have all witnessed at work. They come home to their constituents as lions and return to either their state capitols or the national capital as lambs. They promise to not hide their conservative credentials at home, but lose their credentials when we need them most. We can no longer afford to be represented by those who will lose their will in a fight. We must remove those individuals from office who cannot find the internal strength to do what is right when the pressure is applied. I believe it is important to know how your elected members of the Senate and the U.S. House of Representatives voted.

According to Congress.gov H.R. 2775 – Continuing Appropriations Act, 2014 by the 113th Congress (2013-2014)

List of Senate votes broken down by state

State	Senator 1	Senator 2
Alabama:	Sessions (R-AL), **Nay**	Shelby (R-AL), **Nay**
Alaska:	Begich (D-AK), **Yea**	Murkowski (R-AK), **Yea**
Arizona:	Flake (R-AZ), **Yea**	McCain (R-AZ), **Yea**
Arkansas:	Boozman (R-AR), **Yea**	Pryor (D-AR), **Yea**
California:	Boxer (D-CA), **Yea**	Feinstein (D-CA), **Yea**
Colorado:	Bennet (D-CO), **Yea**	Udall (D-CO), **Yea**
Connecticut:	Blumenthal (D-CT), **Yea**	Murphy (D-CT), **Yea**
Delaware:	Carper (D-DE), **Yea**	Coons (D-DE), **Yea**
Florida:	Nelson (D-FL), **Yea**	Rubio (R-FL), **Nay**
Georgia:	Chambliss (R-GA), **Yea**	Isakson (R-GA), **Yea**
Hawaii:	Hirono (D-HI), **Yea**	Schatz (D-HI), **Yea**
Idaho:	Crapo (R-ID), **Nay**	Risch (R-ID), **Nay**
Illinois:	Durbin (D-IL), **Yea**	Kirk (R-IL), **Yea**
Indiana:	Coats (R-IN), **Yea**	Donnelly (D-IN), **Yea**
Iowa:	Grassley (R-IA), **Nay**	Harkin (D-IA), **Yea**
Kansas:	Moran (R-KS), **Yea**	Roberts (R-KS), **Nay**
Kentucky:	McConnell (R-KY), **Yea**	Paul (R-KY), **Nay**
Louisiana:	Landrieu (D-LA), **Yea**	Vitter (R-LA), **Nay**
Maine:	Collins (R-ME), **Yea**	King (I-ME), **Yea**
Maryland:	Cardin (D-MD), **Yea**	Mikulski (D-MD), **Yea**
Massachusetts:	Markey (D-MA), **Yea**	Warren (D-MA), **Yea**
Michigan:	Levin (D-MI), **Yea**	Stabenow (D-MI), **Yea**
Minnesota:	Franken (D-MN), **Yea**	Klobuchar (D-MN), **Yea**
Mississippi:	Cochran (R-MS), **Yea**	Wicker (R-MS), **Yea**
Missouri:	Blunt (R-MO), **Yea**	McCaskill (D-MO), **Yea**
Montana:	Baucus (D-MT), **Yea**	Tester (D-MT), **Yea**
Nebraska:	Fischer (R-NE), **Yea**	Johanns (R-NE), **Yea**
Nevada:	Heller (R-NV), **Nay**	Reid (D-NV), **Yea**
New Hampshire:	Ayotte (R-NH), **Yea**	Shaheen (D-NH), **Yea**
New Jersey:	Chiesa (R-NJ), **Yea**	Menendez (D-NJ), **Yea**
New Mexico:	Heinrich (D-NM), **Yea**	Udall (D-NM), **Yea**
New York:	Gillibrand (D-NY), **Yea**	Schumer (D-NY), **Yea**
North Carolina:	Burr (R-NC), **Yea**	Hagan (D-NC), **Yea**
North Dakota:	Heitkamp (D-ND), **Yea**	Hoeven (R-ND), **Yea**
Ohio:	Brown (D-OH), **Yea**	Portman (R-OH), **Yea**
Oklahoma:	Coburn (R-OK), **Nay**	Inhofe (R-OK), **Not Voting**
Oregon:	Merkley (D-OR), **Yea**	Wyden (D-OR), **Yea**
Pennsylvania:	Casey (D-PA), **Yea**	Toomey (R-PA), **Nay**
Rhode Island:	Reed (D-RI), **Yea**	Whitehouse (D-RI), **Yea**
South Carolina:	Graham (R-SC), **Yea**	Scott (R-SC), **Nay**
South Dakota:	Johnson (D-SD), **Yea**	Thune (R-SD), **Yea**
Tennessee:	Alexander (R-TN), **Yea**	Corker (R-TN), **Yea**
Texas:	Cornyn (R-TX), **Nay**	Cruz (R-TX), **Nay**
Utah:	Hatch (R-UT), **Yea**	Lee (R-UT), **Nay**
Vermont:	Leahy (D-VT), **Yea**	Sanders (I-VT), **Yea**
Virginia:	Kaine (D-VA), **Yea**	Warner (D-VA), **Yea**
Washington:	Cantwell (D-WA), **Yea**	Murray (D-WA), **Yea**
West Virginia:	Manchin (D-WV), **Yea**	Rockefeller (D-WV), **Yea**
Wisconsin:	Baldwin (D-WI), **Yea**	Johnson (R-WI), **Nay**
Wyoming:	Barrasso (R-WY), **Yea**	Enzi (R-WY), **Nay**

List of House votes broken down by Yeas and Nays:

BILL TITLE: To condition the provision of premium and cost-sharing subsidies under the Patient Protection and Affordable Care Act upon a certification that a program to verify household income and other qualifications for such subsidies is operational, and for other purposes

	YEAS	NAYS	PRES	NV
REPUBLICAN	230			2
DEMOCRATIC	5	191		4
INDEPENDENT				
TOTALS	**235**	**191**		**6**

– YEAS 235 –

Aderholt
Alexander
Amash
Amodei
Bachmann
Bachus
Barletta
Barr
Barrow (GA)
Barton
Benishek
Bentivolio
Bilirakis
Bishop (UT)
Black
Blackburn
Boustany
Brady (TX)
Bridenstine

Brooks (AL)
Brooks (IN)
Broun (GA)
Buchanan
Bucshon
Burgess
Calvert
Camp
Campbell
Cantor
Capito
Carter
Cassidy
Chabot
Chaffetz
Coble
Coffman
Cole
Collins (GA)

Collins (NY)
Conaway
Cook
Cotton
Cramer
Crawford
Crenshaw
Culberson
Daines
Davis, Rodney
Denham
Dent
DeSantis
DesJarlais
Duffy
Duncan (SC)
Duncan (TN)
Ellmers
Farenthold

Fincher
Fitzpatrick
Fleischmann
Fleming
Flores
Forbes
Fortenberry
Foxx
Franks (AZ)
Frelinghuysen
Gardner
Garrett
Gerlach
Gibbs
Gibson
Gingrey (GA)
Gohmert
Goodlatte
Gosar
Gowdy
Granger
Graves (GA)
Graves (MO)
Griffin (AR)
Griffith (VA)
Grimm
Guthrie
Hall
Hanna
Harper
Harris
Hartzler
Hastings (WA)
Heck (NV)
Hensarling
Holding
Hudson
Huelskamp
Huizenga (MI)
Hultgren
Hunter
Hurt
Issa
Jenkins
Johnson (OH)
Johnson, Sam
Jones
Jordan
Joyce
Kelly (PA)
King (IA)
King (NY)
Kingston
Kinzinger (IL)
Kline
Labrador
LaMalfa
Lamborn
Lance
Lankford
Latham
Latta
Lipinski
LoBiondo
Long
Lucas
Luetkemeyer
Lummis
Marchant
Marino
Massie
Matheson
McCarthy (CA)
McCaul
McClintock
McHenry
McIntyre
McKeon
McKinley
McMorris Rodgers
Meadows
Meehan
Messer
Mica
Miller (FL)
Miller (MI)
Miller, Gary
Mullin
Mulvaney
Murphy (PA)
Neugebauer
Noem
Nugent
Nunes
Nunnelee
Olson
Palazzo
Paulsen
Pearce
Perry
Peterson Petri
Pittenger
Pitts
Poe (TX)
Pompeo
Posey
Price (GA)
Radel
Reed
Reichert
Renacci
Ribble
Rice (SC)
Rigell

Roby
Roe (TN)
Rogers (AL)
Rogers (KY)
Rogers (MI)
Rohrabacher
Rokita
Rooney
Ros-Lehtinen
Roskam
Ross
Rothfus
Royce
Runyan
Ryan (WI)
Salmon
Sanford
Scalise
Schock
Schweikert
Scott, Austin

Sensenbrenner
Sessions
Shimkus
Shuster
Simpson
Smith (MO)
Smith (NE)
Smith (NJ)
Smith (TX)
Southerland
Stewart
Stivers
Stockman
Stutzman
Terry
Thompson (PA)
Thornberry
Tiberi
Tipton
Turner
Upton

Valadao
Wagner
Walberg
Walden
Walorski
Weber (TX)
Webster (FL)
Wenstrup
Westmoreland
Whitfield
Williams
Wilson (SC)
Wittman
Wolf
Womack
Woodall
Yoder
Yoho
Young (AK)
Young (FL)
Young (IN)

– NAYS 191 –

Andrews
Barber
Bass
Beatty
Becerra
Bera (CA)
Bishop (GA)
Bishop (NY)
Blumenauer
Bonamici
Brady (PA)
Braley (IA)
Brown (FL)

Brownley (CA)
Bustos
Butterfield
Capps
Capuano
Cárdenas
Carney
Carson (IN)
Cartwright
Castor (FL)
Castro (TX)
Chu
Cicilline

Clarke
Clay
Cleaver
Clyburn
Cohen
Connolly
Conyers
Cooper
Costa
Courtney
Crowley
Cuellar
Cummings

Davis (CA)
Davis, Danny
DeFazio
DeGette
Delaney
DeLauro
DelBene
Deutch
Dingell
Doggett
Doyle
Duckworth
Edwards
Ellison
Engel
Enyart
Eshoo
Esty
Farr
Fattah
Foster
Frankel (FL)
Fudge
Gabbard
Gallego
Garamendi
Garcia
Grayson
Green, Al
Green, Gene
Grijalva
Gutiérrez
Hahn
Hanabusa
Hastings (FL)
Heck (WA)
Higgins
Himes
Hinojosa
Holt
Honda
Horsford
Hoyer
Huffman
Israel
Jackson Lee
Jeffries
Johnson (GA)
Johnson, E. B.
Kaptur
Keating
Kelly (IL)
Kennedy
Kildee
Kilmer
Kind
Kirkpatrick
Kuster
Langevin
Larsen (WA)
Larson (CT)
Lee (CA)
Levin
Lewis
Loebsack
Lofgren
Lowenthal
Lowey
Lujan
Grisham (NM)
Luján,
Ben Ray (NM)
Lynch
Maffei
Maloney, Carolyn
Maloney, Sean
Matsui
McCollum
McDermott
McGovern
McNerney
Meeks
Meng
Michaud
Miller, George
Moore
Moran
Murphy (FL)
Napolitano
Neal
Negrete McLeod
Nolan
O'Rourke
Owens
Pallone
Pascrell
Pastor (AZ)
Payne
Pelosi
Perlmutter
Peters (CA)
Peters (MI)
Pingree (ME)
Pocan
Polis
Price (NC)
Quigley
Rahall
Rangel
Richmond
Roybal-Allard
Ruiz
Ruppersberger
Ryan (OH)

Sánchez, Linda T.	Sinema	Vargas
Sanchez, Loretta	Sires	Veasey
Sarbanes	Slaughter	Vela
Schakowsky	Smith (WA)	Velázquez
Schiff	Speier	Walz
Schneider	Swalwell (CA)	Wasserman Schultz
Schrader	Takano	Waters
Schwartz	Thompson (CA)	Watt
Scott (VA)	Thompson (MS)	Waxman
Scott, David	Tierney	Welch
Serrano	Titus	Wilson (FL)
Sewell (AL)	Tonko	Yarmuth
Shea-Porter	Tsongas	
Sherman	Van Hollen	

– NOT VOTING 6 –

Diaz-Balart	*McCarthy (NY)*	*Rush*
Herrera Beutler	*Nadler*	*Visclosky*

Did your elected congressman or senator vote in your best interest or theirs? We must immediately begin to hold those we elect strictly accountable for their behavior. Our government is here to represent us and yes, even fear us if they don't represent properly. For far too long elected officials have been treated as though they were rock stars instead of public "servants". We must let those who do not honor our values move on because we can't afford to keep electing them.

I would be remiss if I did not mention one of my states Senators and I'm only going to mention one. Ted Cruz of Texas ran for U.S. Senate as a Tea Party Conservative. Ted Cruz on more occasions than I can count publicly stated that if elected he would do everything he could to defund Obamacare. I spent a great deal of time around Ted and his message was clear and consistent. Now we have all heard candidates and elected officials promise to do this or that, but how often have we seen one knock it out of the park. Ted Cruz stood tall and pushed "hard" even against establishment Republicans in his attempt to defund Obamacare. Now whether you like Senator Cruz or not, how can you possible not like a politician who runs on an issue and then does exactly what he promised.

None of us should like the old bait and switch tactic used by candidates and elected officials. How Arizona keeps sending John McCain back to the U. S. Senate is a mystery to me. McCain has demonstrated again and again that he will bend too far "left" and for me that doesn't work!

The slogan "Let's take our country back" means exactly that. Sad to say we have to take it back from some who claimed to be with us! The motto of the United States Marine Corps is "Semper Fidelis" Latin for "Always Faithful". This is the mandate that we should all hold our elected representatives to.

Chapter 27

HOW REPUBLICANS WIN

"History has demonstrated that the most notable winners usually encountered heartbreaking obstacles before they triumphed. They won because they refused to become discouraged by their defeats." (Forbes 2014)" – **Bertie C. Forbes**

1. Clearly define ourselves and communicate who we are and not allow anyone else to define us.
2. Clearly communicate what we believe, don't believe and why.
3. Clearly demonstrate our true passion to help those who **cannot** help themselves.
    a. Elderly and Seniors
    b. Very young and those in need of temporary assistance. It can happen to anyone of us.
    c. Mentally & Developmentally Disabled
4. Establish a strong, yet sensible immigration policy that is favorable towards the compliant and punitive towards the violators.

5. Be honest and transparent in all of our dealings by holding fellow Republicans accountable for bad behavior, so we can have support when holding Democrats accountable. Let's call things what they are and stop beating around the bush!
6. Set up mentoring for underprivileged youth to show them the advantages of work.
7. Honor our commitments to those who have honored their commitments, retirees and military veterans.
8. Grow our party through outreach without compromising our values, but step out of the old comfort zones. Let's quit telling people why they should be conservative Republicans and show them why! Let our actions speak loudly!
9. Let's educate the new younger generation and show them why it is to their benefit to adopt conservative values and principles. Find young, conservative-leaning minorities and help groom them for public office through an apprentice-based mentoring program.
10. Bring our Christian values to the forefront of what we do and share it always.

Chapter 28

MY FAITH

"But whosoever shall deny me before men, him will I also deny before my Father which is in heaven"
—Matthew 10:33

As a child my mother did something very important. She didn't send us to church, she took us to church. I will never forget Sunday school at 8:30 AM and then regular services at 10:00 AM. As a child time seemed to stop in church because those Sunday mornings would turn into late afternoon. There was really no set time that church could end, but we would generally be dismissed around 1:00pm. I remember my mother would tell us that if we could sit and watch a television for four or five hours, then we could give that much time to Jesus on Sunday.

I accepted Jesus Christ as my Lord and Savior when I was seven years old. I think as a child I went to alter call because I was afraid of what was waiting if I did not. We attended Thomas Memorial Church of God in Christ and our Pastor, Reverend Dixon, was a fire and brimstone preacher. I can remember

My Faith

thinking, "who would ever want to take the chance of ending up in hell? " There are many reasons that you may choose to accept Jesus Christ as your Lord and Savior, but the only thing that matters is that you accept Him.

I know that Jesus Christ died for me on the cross at Calvary. The knowledge that regardless of whatever has to be endured here on earth is temporary, but the gift of heaven is eternal. I have often heard my current pastor, Tommy Burchfield of Believer's World Outreach Church say, "Eternity is too long, to get it wrong!" For those who don't believe, I hope and pray for them all that they find and seek the forgiveness of God.

Forgiveness is what I needed from God, but it took me a long time to learn to forgive. Forgiveness is for yourself, not for the person who may have wronged you. During my race for Sheriff there were people attacking me and my family and doing and saying some of the most hateful things imaginable. I won't tell you that it wasn't upsetting, but I will tell you that my faith in God and my ability to forgive, by His grace, is what got me through without responding in kind.

Many believe that they cannot stand tall against adversity; it is not always important that you stand tall, but you must always find the strength to stand up!

I know that whenever this journey ends, I get to go home to meet the Father. The knowledge that there is eternal peace and I can share in it is a very comforting thought.

I wrote the following poem after a very long day and it just came to me so I wanted to share it with all of you.

God is always watching;
He doesn't need to sleep; each and every promise
he will surely keep
The gifts of heaven are plenty
The reality of hell is real
Don't sacrifice your eternal reward
In an attempt to please man's ideals
We must each stand before the Father
And answer for our deeds
His promise of acceptance and forgiveness
is all we truly need
No one will live forever
Judgment Day shall surely come
Be not tardy, asking forgiveness, for all that you have done
May God hold you close
So close you do not roam
I pray that he safely guide you all the way back home

CLOSING

In looking back over my now 50 years of life I am happy that God has seen fit to bless me with a family and extended family that loves me, and career(s) that have allowed me to make a difference. Family, Faith and Country have always been the most important things in my life. We have a choice in who we are, what we do and how we treat one another. This great nation we call home was founded in faith and I believe that God still has further plans for us, but the further we, as a nation, have moved away from God the worse things have gotten and will continue to get. I will continue being a common sense conservative voice for truth because "right is right and wrong is wrong, no matter who does it!"

The devil is real and to our eternal benefit; so is God. The time for us to pray is not during battle, but before the battle begins.

The End

It will end with

GOD

BIBLIOGRAPHY

2011. http://www.tuskegeeairmennationalmuseum.org/ (accessed November 30, 2013).

Abrahamson, Alan. "Fuhrman Grants Interview, Apologizes for Slurs." *Los Angeles Times*, October 8, 1996.

Adams, John. *John Adams Quotes on Government.* n.d. http://www.john-adams-heritage.com/quotes/ (accessed November 30, 2013).

Armour, Richard. *Learning right from left from wrong.* 2013. http://www.dailycomet.com/article/20121104/OPINION01/121109866 (accessed November 30, 2013).

Attributed to Thatcher, Margaret. *Talk:Margaret Thatcher.* December 27, 2013. http://en.wikiquote.org/wiki/Talk:Margaret_Thatcher (accessed Novembe 30, 2013).

Bartlett, Bruce. *Whitewash-The racist history the Democratic Party wants you to forget.* December 24, 2007. http://online.wsj.com/news/articles/SB122513867582273213 (accessed March 15, 2014).

Belew, Noah H. *The Few, the Proud.* n.d. http://www.semperfidelisnoah.com/TheFewTheProud.htm (accessed November 30, 2013).

Berton, Pierre. *Racism is a refuge for the ignorant. It seeks to divide and to destroy. It is the enemy of freedom, and deserves to be met head-on and stamped out.* n.d. http://www.brainyquote.com/quotes/quotes/p/pierrebert177805.html (accessed November 30, 2013).

Burke, Attributed to Edmund. *Quote Investigator.* December 4, 2010. http://quoteinvestigator.com/2010/12/04/good-men-do/ (accessed November 30, 2013).

California Republican Party Gaylord Parkinson. 1966. http://en.wikipedia.org/wiki/The_Eleventh_Commandment_(Ronald_Reagan) (accessed November 1, 2013).

Caro, Robert A. *Master of the Senate: The Years of Lyndon Johnson III.* 2003.

Carroll, Attributed mistakenly to Lewis. *Lenny's Alice in Wonderland Site.* May 27, 2008. http://www.alice-in-wonderland.net/books/alice-in-wonderland-quotes.html (accessed November 30, 2013).

Center for Responsive Politics. n.d. (accessed November 30, 2013).

—. n.d. (accessed November 30, 2013).

—. n.d. (accessed November 30, 2013).

—. n.d. (accessed Novembe 30, 2013).

—. *Personal Finances.* n.d. http://www.opensecrets.org/pfds/ (accessed November 30, 2013).

Chumley, Cheryl K. *Rep. Sheila Jackson Lee claims Constitution is 400 years old.* March 13, 2014. http://www.washingtontimes.com/news/2014/mar/13/sheila-jackson-lee-claims-constitution-400-years-o/ (accessed March 15, 2014).

Bibliography

Churchill, Winston. ""True Origin Unknown"." *Finest Hour, The Journal of Winston Churchill*, Winter 2009-2010: 9.

Churchill, Winston. "True Origin Unknown." *Finest Hour, The Journal of Winston Churchill*, Winter 2009-2010: 9.

—. *Winston Churchill quotes.* n.d. http://quotes4all.net/winston%20churchill.html (accessed November 30, 2013).

CNN Political Unit. *Americans divided over Zimmerman verdict, poll finds.* July 22, 2013. http://politicalticker.blogs.cnn.com/2013/07/22/americans-divided-over-zimmerman-verdict-poll-finds/?iref=allsearch (accessed November 30, 2013).

Confucius, Attributed to. *Confucius Quotes.* n.d. http://www.searchquotes.com/search/Confucius/2/ (accessed November 30, 2013).

Data Brief: Black Employment and Unemployment December 2012. January 4, 2013. http://laborcenter.berkeley.edu/blackworkers/monthly/bwreport_2013-01-04_56.pdf (accessed November 30, 2013).

Dr. David Pilgrim, Professor of Sociology. *Jim Crow Museum of Racist Memorabilia.* 2012. http://www.ferris.edu/jimcrow/what.htm (accessed November 30, 2013).

Einstein, Albert. *The definition of "insanity" is the most overused cliché of all time.* August 6, 2013. http://www.salon.com/2013/08/06/the_definition_of_insanity_is_the_most_overused_cliche_of_all_time/ (accessed November 30, 2013).

Eisenhower and the Little Rock Crisis. n.d. http://www.americaslibrary.gov/aa/eisenhower/aa_eisenhower_littlerock_3.html (accessed November 30, 2013).

Forbes, Bertie C. *B. C. Forbes Quotes.* January 10, 2014. http://www.loveaquote.com/authors/b-c-forbes-quotes/ (accessed November 30, 2013).

Former Sheriff Guilty in Successor's Killing. 11 2002, July. http://www.nytimes.com/2002/07/11/us/former-sheriff-guilty-in-successor-s-killing.html?ref=sidney_dorsey (accessed November 30, 2013).

Goodman, Benny. *Some quotes by, and about Benny Goodman.* January 15, 2013. http://bennygdog.blogspot.com/2013/01/some-quotes-by-and-about-benny-goodman.html (accessed November 30, 2013).

Guttmacher Institute. *Facts on Induced Abortion in the United States.* December 2013. http://www.guttmacher.org/pubs/fb_induced_abortion.html (accessed November 30, 2013).

Henry, Patrick. *Patrick Henry Quotes.* n.d. http://www.finestquotes.com/author_quotes-author-Patrick%20Henry-page-0.htm (accessed November 30, 2013).

Huffington Post. *The Democratic Party's Two-Facedness of Race Relations.* August 24, 2011. http://www.huffingtonpost.com/the-relentless-conservative/the-democratic-partys-two_b_933995.html (accessed March 15, 2014).

Jackson, Kevin. *Reid–Racist Revisionist.* 2009. http://theblacksphere.net/2009/12/reid-racist-revisionist/ (accessed March 15, 2014).

Japanese proverbs. November 12, 2013. http://en.wikipedia.org/wiki/Japanese_proverbs (accessed November 30, 2013).

Jefferson, Thomas. *A Little Rebellion Now and Then Is A Good Thing A Letter From Thomas Jefferson To James Madison.*

January 30, 1787. http://www.earlyamerica.com/review/summer/letter.html (accessed November 30, 2013).

—. *Home › Jefferson › Quotations › Famous Quotations.* n.d. http://www.monticello.org/site/jefferson/wasting-labours-people-quotation (accessed November 30, 2013).

—. *Home › Jefferson › Quotations › Famous Quotations.* n.d. http://www.monticello.org/site/jefferson/wasting-labours-people-quotation (accessed November 30, 2013).

King, Jr., Martin Luther. *Editorial: Martin Luther King Jr. Day quotes 2014.* January 20, 2014. http://www.nj.com/times-opinion/index.ssf/2014/01/opinion_martin_luther_king_jr.html (accessed November 30, 2013).

KKK Terrorist Arm of the Democratic Party. 2009. http://www.nationalblackrepublicans.com/index.cfm?fuseaction=pages.DYKKKKTerroristArmoftheDemocratParty (accessed November 30, 2013).

Maxwell, John C. *The Right to Lead: Learning Leadership Through Character and Courage.* Thomas Nelson, 2010.

McMurran, Kristin. *A California Highway Patrolman Is Tried Once Again for a Shocking Murder Under the Freeway.* June 13, 1988. http://www.people.com/people/archive/article/0,,20099196,00.html (accessed November 30, 2013).

Pepper (D., Fla.), 1938, Senator Claude. *Reid – Racist Revisionist.* 2009. http://theblacksphere.net/2009/12/reid-racist-revisionist/ (accessed 03 15, 2014).

Petrillo, Lisa. *The Killer Cop.* February 2004. http://www.sandiegomagazine.com/San-Diego-Magazine/February-2004/The-Killer-Cop/ (accessed November 30, 2013).

Picasso, Pablo. *Pablo Picass oPaintings, Quotes, and Biography.* n.d. http://www.pablopicasso.org/quotes.jsp (accessed November 30, 2013).

Politico Staff. *Election 2012: See full results.* January 10, 2013. http://www.politico.com/2012-election/ (accessed November 30, 2013).

Preston, Julia, and John H. Cushman Jr. *Obama to Permit Young Migrants to Remain in U.S.* June 15, 2012. http://www.nytimes.com/2012/06/16/us/us-to-stop-deporting-some-illegal-immigrants.html?pagewanted=all&_r=0 (accessed November 30, 2013).

Reagan, Ronald. *Address to the annual meeting of the Phoenix Chamber of Commerce.* Performed by Ronald Reagan. Address to the annual meeting of the Phoenix Chamber of Commerce, Phoenix, AZ. March 30, 1967.

Rodney King, key L.A. riots figure, dead at 47. June 17, 2012. http://latimesblogs.latimes.com/lanow/2012/06/rodney-king-whose-beating-by-los-angeles-police-helped-spark-the-1992-los-angeles-riots-died-sunday-at-his-home-in-rialto.html (accessed November 30, 2013).

ROE V. WADE. 70-18 (Supreme Court, January 22, 1973).

Rogers, Will. *Will Rogers Quotes.* September 30, 1923. http://www.notable-quotes.com/r/rogers_will.html (accessed November 30, 2013).

Roosevelt, Theodore. *Search Quotes.* n.d. http://www.searchquotes.com/quotation/When_they_call_the_roll_in_the_Senate,_the_Senators_do_not_know_whether_to_answer_Present_or_Not_gui/200222/ (accessed November 30, 2013).

Sandburg, Carl. *Quotes.* n.d. http://www.quotery.com/a-baby-is-gods-opinion-that-life-should-go-on/ (accessed November 30, 2013).

Sharpton, Al. *National Action Network » About.* 2011. http://nationalactionnetwork.net/about/ (accessed November 30, 2013).

Spetalnick, Matt, and Steve Holland. *Obama tells Russia's Medvedev more flexibility after election.* March 28, 2012. http://www.reuters.com/article/2012/03/26/us-nuclear-summit-obama-medvedev-idUSBRE82P0JI20120326 (accessed November 30, 2013).

Tapper, Jake. *Michelle Obama: "For the First Time in My Adult Lifetime, I'm Really Proud of My Country".* February 18, 2008. http://abcnews.go.com/blogs/politics/2008/02/michelle-obam-1-2/ (accessed November 30, 2013).

Taylor, Robert Lewis. *W.C. Fields: His Follies and Fortunes.* Doubleday & Co., 1949.

Thatcher, Margaret. *Speech.* Performed by Margaret Thatcher. Royal Albert Hall, London. May 20, 1965.

The Associated Press. *Jury convicts ex-HPD officer Drew Ryser of official oppression in Chad Holley beating case.* June 12, 2013. http://abclocal.go.com/ktrk/story?section=news/local&id=9136131 (accessed November 30, 2013).

The Debt to the Penny and Who Holds It. January 22, 2014. http://www.treasurydirect.gov/NP/debt/current (accessed November 30, 2013).

The Niagara Movement. January 10, 2014. http://en.wikipedia.org/wiki/Niagara_Movement (accessed November 30, 2013).

The Niagra Movement. January 10, 2014. http://en.wikipedia.org/wiki/Niagara_Movement (accessed November 30, 2013).

The Niagra Movement. January 10, 2014. http://en.wikipedia.org/wiki/Niagara_Movement (accessed November 30, 2013).

The Niagra Movement. January 10, 2014. http://en.wikipedia.org/wiki/Niagara_Movement (accessed November 30, 2013).

The Niagra Movement. January 10, 2014. http://en.wikipedia.org/wiki/Niagara_Movement (accessed November 30, 2013).

The Niagra Movement. January 10, 2014. http://en.wikipedia.org/wiki/Niagara_Movement (accessed November 30, 2013).

"U.S. Army Center of Military History." *Title 10, US Code; Act of 5 May 1960.* May 5, 1960.

Urban Institute, Brookings Institution, . *Tax Policy Center 2011.* n.d. http://www.taxpolicycenter.org/taxtopics/federal-taxes-households.cfm (accessed November 30, 2013).

Sands of Iwo Jima. Directed by Allan Dwan. Performed by John Wayne as Sgt. John M. Stryker. 1949.

Sands of Iwo Jima. Directed by Allan Dwan. Performed by John Wayne as Sgt. John M. Stryker. 1949.

Sands of Iwo Jima. Directed by Allan Dwan. Performed by John Wayne as Sgt. John M. Stryker. 1949.

www.juneteenth.com. n.d. http://www.juneteenth.com/ (accessed November 30, 2013).